Going Against the Grain is a collaborative masterpiece providing wisdom, insight and education to future pioneering trailblazers and a must read for those who care about the future of leadership. In 33 years of being in the leadership trenches I have had the privilege to meet visionary thought leaders who have ambitious legacies and who are making a significant difference on this planet of ours – entrée Cathy Dimarchos, who's servant leadership, heart, vision and legacy is nothing short of extraordinary. Her selfless contribution is to be admired. To achieve a legacy of the magnitude Cathy aspires, requires her to leverage her co-creative ability to be called to a vision of this nature. This calling can only be sourced from a deep spiritual foundation.

> – Sally Anderson
> Leadership Coach To The Influencers
> https://www.linkedin.com/in/sallyanderson-leadershipcoachtotheinfluencers/

This is an inspirational anthology of compelling personal stories from women who share their individual experiences and life lessons. Sometimes looking at successful and accomplished people makes hard to imagine that their path was not smooth. These incredible women had all their own path by persevering against insurmountable odds and going forward in spite of personal setbacks. Each woman's story contains powerful lessons that are relatable and encouraging that give you a sense of camaraderie and motivation. A great read for anyone who is seeking guidance and inspiration to overcome adversity and find your inner strength and purpose. I thoroughly enjoyed reading and learning about these amazing women and their life stories.

> – Naidira Alemova, Senior Managing Director,
> FTI Consulting in New York, USA

*Going Against The Grain* is a comprehensive, thought-provoking page-turner which takes the reader on a journey of self-discovery – not just by providing helpful tools that encourage curiosity and introspection but also by showcasing real-life examples. Gabby's willingness to be candid and vulnerable in telling her story allows us to ‹pull the curtain aside› and witness a beautifully relatable transformation. She shares her inner knowledge, understanding and life experience in this masterful book that will enrich readers' lives in numerous ways. Don't pass this book by; it's well worth your time.

– Kirsty Ogden, Brisbane

A true leader does more than manage others. They inspire other individuals to reach their highest potentials. Gabby's contribution Discovering My Authenticity in the wonderful collaborative work Going Against The Grain, is a very powerful focus of growth, change, and leadership. Gabby is a courageous catalyst to ignite the potential within from her own life experiences and powerfully in those who are called to work with her. An integral read for anyone to elevate their intelligent, emotional and spiritual path.

– Lynne Smith Astrology
Astrologer | Teacher | Mentor | Writer

**If you're looking for a better understanding of how your mindset affects your opinions,** self-worth, outlook on the world, personal limitations and the trajectory of your life, Going Against The Grain is an discerning read. Gabby's insights into the world of Astrology and its influence to follow her authenticity inspires the reader to reach beyond their dreams. If you want to learn more about yourself and those around you, this book will be a great investment in your success.

– Lisa Lindsay – Brisbane

The world has very set opinions on what is "right" and "wrong". Going against the grain of these opinions makes for interesting stories, and that's what Cathy's book Going against the grain is about. Cathy's book "Going against the grain" is a collection of stories about different women who chose to do things their own way, against the grain of society. Each of these women had to overcome difficulty, navigate new territory, and learn new things to make it happen.

I thoroughly enjoyed reading about the choices each woman had to make, and challenges they met as they sought to follow their own path. I also love that this book also shares the stories of different women who are not just strangers but rather, have become friends because of the choices they have made together. Thankyou Cathy for helping us to embrace difference, encourage freedom of expression, and motivate everyone to make a positive impact on the world around them through this book

     – Hazel Herrington
     Marketing and Brand Creation Expert
     Founder, Herrington Publications Worldwide

# GOING AGAINST THE GRAIN

*Compiled by*
Cathy Dimarchos

Edited by Tracy Regan

Typeset in Adobe Garamond Pro 12/17pt by New Dawn Publishing Pty Ltd

 A catalogue record for this work is available from the National Library of Australia

NATIONAL LIBRARY OF AUSTRALIA

National Library of Australia Catalogue-in-Publication data:
Going Against the Grain/Cathy Dimarchos

ISBN: 978-0-6453319-4-3
(Paperback)

ISBN: 978-0-6453319-5-0
(Ebook)

# CONTENTS

# INTRODUCTION

At the centre of everything we do are people. We all have something to say, an opinion, a way in which we do things, but so very often we hold back and fall in line with what everyone around is doing for fear of standing out, being seen as different, or even being judged.

However, it is this uniqueness that draws people to one another. The ability to be authentic, to be vulnerable and to be confident in being you. So, this collaboration is to share our stories and show others they can do it too.

The world is evolving at such a rapid pace and our future generation is thinking beyond now, in fact they are thinking beyond self and to things across the globe. We want to encourage them to think big, think limitlessly and to go against the grain.

This book is dedicated to our future generations, and to all of you who dare to dream to be different, and who dare to do things your way. I encourage each of you to stay true to you, to step up, to show up and to take others with you.

The amazing humans whom I have carefully selected to join me on this journey have been brought together from across the globe. Each of them has crossed my path from different areas of my life, from trekking with gorilla's in Uganda, whilst others I have met through visits to Tanzania and being embraced as part of a family, to being asked for feedback and guidance in starting up a new business, to being part of entrepreneur programs, being engaged as a business advisor to meeting on as I began my speaking engagement journey on stage.

All have alignment in values and in purpose, most importantly they have had the courage and conviction to do things their way. Their commitment and determination to live life to the fullest and to bring others on the journey with them is what drew me to them.

They now form part of my inner circle and it is a privilege to call them my friends.

Remember the path forward is the one you choose for you. It does not need to be straight; it doesn't need to have twists and turns; it just needs to be the one for you. Step forward into the world being exactly who you were meant to be. Do things your way and take others with you and most importantly elevate those around you.

For me my journey in life has begun a new circle, one that is dedicated to sharing knowledge and showing others the power of paying things forward. I choose to step forward knowing the impact that I can create by elevating others. I have committed to raising the baseline of where people begin to live life and am on a mission to find like-minded people who will share this journey with me.

As the founder of Solutions2You, my mission is to pay

things forward and whilst I love the work that I do in scaling businesses and coaching executives across the globe, I know that my end game is to pay things forward through the leadership programs that we have developed. I have called this project Raise the Baseline, and it is dedicated to developing our future generations starting with children as young as 12 years of age. The programs range in age groups 12-14, 15-17, and then school leavers (2 programs, one for those who choose a path to become self-employed and the other for those who choose a career as an employee).

Our programs inspire, elevate and encourage children to self-regulate, find true purpose and develop skills as future leaders so that they can contribute to the changes that they want to see in the world, in their communities and within themselves. Most importantly they develop courage to embrace differences so that they may better understand the world we live in.

The proceeds of this book contribute to the leadership programs under the Raise the Baseline Programs running in underdeveloped countries. Whilst we have started in Tanzania, it is something we will expand globally so we are looking for like-minded people to support us on our journey. Australia will be launching these programs for aspiring young leaders in 2022.

I want to show my gratitude to each of the authors in this book who have had faith in me and my purpose in paying things forward. Most importantly they had faith in taking their path forward in being the amazing humans that they are.

If there is one thing I know and can share, is that each of them have begun their next stage in actualisation, as their story here in this book is just the beginning of where they are going.

Thank you to Karen Mc Dermott who not only is a co-author but also publishing this book. Her magic is what brings us all together.

'Being bold and being prepared leads to opportunities that when actioned will deliver an incredible outcome. I truly believe this and encourage you to share your journey with me.

We all have many sides to ourselves and yes, we can be all of them! Live and enjoy life in all that is has to offer ... challenges and victories.'

– Cathy Dimarchos

# RESILIENCE, COURAGE AND GETTING THINGS DONE TOGETHER

*Belinda Wera*

M y dad was born and raised in a small village called Ng'uni on the slopes of Mount Kilimanjaro, the highest mountain in Africa, 5,895 meters above sea level. He was named Jubilant. Jubilant! 'Where did that name came from?' I asked my dad, knowing my grandparents did not speak English. He told me my grandfather worked for the colonialists and that's how he encountered the English language. I think from when he was born my grandparents could see how jovial and happy my dad was, and he lives up to his name. Dad can charm his way through any situation! Born into a family of 8, dad was the seventh born and second male child. He claims to be grandma's favourite – but aren't we all.

Dad loved school. Growing up he told us many stories of how he had to work hard balancing education with taking care of his goats and chickens, and cleaning the cow shed every morning. The funniest story he shared was how he wore grandma's shoes to school because he didn't have any of his own. At some point, he outgrew the shoes and had to sell his chickens to buy his own. Thinking about this now, it's not funny at all. He was striving for what he wanted against all odds. It did not matter if he was in his mother's shoes doing it. Hurray! Dad was the first and only child in his family who made it to university. He moved to Arusha town where he had a small retail business to get money for college.

Having worked for the government in the tourism sector for over 10 years, in 2001 dad opened his tour company called Park East Africa; a family-run tour operator business. This company has been a foundation for me to see, learn and build office skills, working there during school holidays.

Mama was born and raised in Machame; a village at the foot of Mount Kilimanjaro. She was the second born and the first girl in the family of 8. That meant she was officially a 'deputy parent'. Being older meant she had the responsibility to nurture her siblings. With those responsibilities, she was very fortunate to still be able to attend school. At the time, school was mainly for the boys in the family, but my grandpa saw something special in his daughter. Mama attended primary school and before long she was relieved of her deputy parental duties to move to Arusha town and live with her uncle who was a medical doctor. Mama's uncle also saw something special in her and knew she needed to move from the village so she could realise her potential. At the age of 17, mama got a job as a computer clerk at the Tanganyika Farmers Association. This was 1978 and the operating system MS-DOS.

My parents had 4 children. Their first born is my only brother, my older sister and my twin sister. I considered myself a middle child for the longest time, as there was really nothing special about me. My brother was mama's prized possession, my sister was dad's little princess and my twin is still the baby of the family. Did I mention that she is my twin? Now you know why I considered myself a middle child. I was trusted with the house chores and mama would always leave the house under my care when she went to work. It wouldn't matter if my older brother and sister were home or not. As she walked towards the door, mama would call out, 'Belinda, I am leaving now, take care of things okay.' That meant ensuring the house was clean, clothes were washed, the garden cleaned, vegetables and flowers watered, and food cooked.

My brother opened his small secretarial office just after he finished high school. This was the first place I learned how to use a computer. He hired my twin and I as interns, where he paid us in kind. He taught us how to use a computer, burn CDs, type and use Microsoft Publisher to create greeting and business cards. He also taught us how to manage customers and upsell more than one service. When I later worked in customer service training, I was more empathetic because I had the experience of managing customers from a young age.

My sister was full of life, she loved mathematics and reading books. She helped us with homework and to prepare for exams. She played with us and created short plays where we were characters. To make the part we tried on her clothes and makeup, which made us feel very grown up. She saved her pocket money and took us for ice cream and shopping during the holidays. My sister travelled the world with my dad. Her bags were always packed with clothes for all weather. Her quest to see the world landed her in Bowling Green State University, in the United States, where she went on to pursue her Masters in Economics.

My twin sister is naturally creative, and loves beauty, fashion and everything art. From the age of 18, she started selling hair, making surplus money from her job as a sales and office administrator in a security company. She used her failures as stepping-stones, as with one business failure she saw an opportunity to open another. In 2016 she was involved in an accident that grounded her for over a year, unfortunately losing her job. She used that time to recover and re-invent herself. While still on crutches she opened a tailor shop from her living room; a business that kept her afloat for 3 years until May 2020 and due to the effect of the pandemic, sadly had to close. Eight months later my twin opened 3 other businesses selling vintage thrift clothing and accessories, events management, and social media pages' management.

I had a happy and lively childhood. Every morning and evening mama made sure we all gathered in the living room to pray together and share a meal. Over the dinner table, we would talk about what we learned in school and our parents would share how the day was at work for them. The last Saturday of the month was time for 'general cleanliness' as mama called it. That day there was no escape. We had an early breakfast; one person cooked a meal that we would eat from lunch to dinner, that way we had enough time to take care of the house. 'The grass is greener where it is watered people, let's go!' That was mama's cue for us to head out to mow the lawn and prune the flowers. There was great teamwork and division of labour. Mama outlined what was to be done for the day and assigned tasks. All the heavy lifting and tasking work was assigned to my dad and brother – cleaning, raking and cooking were for the girls. At the end of the day, mama would buy us soft drinks and tell us why it was important to take care of our house. She checked in to see how we felt looking at our house after the clean up. After that we would sing to gospel or dad would tell us stories as he made a barbeque.

I was fortunate to be exposed to a lot of things from a young age. Looking at the different path my siblings and I took made me believe that each of us has our own path. At school, I was an average B student. I was liked by my teachers for finishing work on time, my positive attitude, and my quest to volunteer and participate in extra-curricular activities. I also took leadership positions in class and school in general. I found myself in shock when I failed my final class 7 examination. This exam determined my education life. I remember sobbing for days. It did not matter that I was on the waiting list for a second selection to join a government school. In my books I had failed, how did this happen? I was smart, I got As, mostly Bs, and a few Cs in primary school. Not wanting to wait, my parents took me to a private school, where I passed the interview and started secondary school.

I encountered another disappointment 4 years later when I got a division 3 at the national exam! Having the time of my life in secondary school I was sure I was going to get a division 2 at least. Although I had passed this time, I had failed in my standards. I remember crying for hours, I vowed to get a division one in high school. I was allocated to join Bwiru Girls High School, a government school in the lake region, but my parents felt I was too young to go so far from home alone. They took me to a Catholic Girls school in Arusha, the town we lived in. Little did they know I was going to Mwanza in 2 years for university.

In high school, I was the school secretary, the second most senior position in the student government. I was responsible for managing student affairs, school cleanliness, and ensuring we had enough meals served on time. My major goal here was to get a division one in the final national exam. We had monthly tests where, at the end of every month, they posted the best 10 and last 5 students for each class. In our first exam I was number 4 in the class. I made it my mission to study strategically with the best in the class, especially those who were smarter than me. I learned from them and found things to teach them as well. I also did things I liked; netball, singing in the school choir, and drama sessions. Lo and behold, I got a division one in my high school and I was overjoyed. My dream and hard work had paid off.

At university, I initially applied for a Bachelors Degree in Mass Communications. This was not an easy choice because, at the time, I still couldn't answer who I wanted to be when I grew up. Yes, I had a division one, but what was I to do with it now? I remembered I had wanted to be many things growing; a teacher because I loved my teachers or a doctor because I wanted to save lives. This dream died quickly when I was admitted to hospital. I knew right then it would be hard for me to be with sick people all day. I also wanted to be a musician. My mama clearly stated it would not happen under her roof! Haha! I also wanted to be a journalist. I remember admiring the news anchors. I would imitate them in my theatrical sessions after the family dinners, or the drama sessions with my sisters. Long story short, in my first year of university I ended up doing two courses to get enough exposure and make an informed decision. When I finally went to the vice-chancellor of the university to request permission to drop Mass Communication and study Public Relations and Marketing he was amazed by my determination, as what I did was abnormal. He encouraged me to go for what I wanted, not fearing to ask and knowing it was okay to change my mind. Three degrees later, I couldn't agree with him more.

In my MBA class we were required to select leaders; the class president, and vice president. When it was time for the selection I nominated myself for the class president role, whilst another gentleman advised that he wanted to be president. To simplify the process because two people were needed, one guy said the gentleman should be president and I should be his vice because I was a woman. I immediately reminded the class I wanted to be president or nothing at all. They later had to vote and I had a landslide victory, missing only 2 votes out of 25. I stood up for myself and used my voice believing I could lead the class. I also knew it meant I was able to network and make connections.

I started my first job as an intern at the East African Community Secretariat (EAC); an intergovernmental organisation composed of 6 countries in the African Great Lakes region in eastern Africa. I always wanted to work for an international organisation. It was 11 am on Wednesday September 28 when I went to EAC Headquarters and asked to see the director of HR. I did not have an appointment, but I went anyway. Luckily he was able to see me and we had a chat. A week later I received an internship position for 3 months. 2 months on, I got my first contract.

Three years later, after working in public relations, I felt it was time for a change. I knew I had potential that needed to be unleashed. In search of something new, I applied and made it into President Obama's youth program; the prestigious Mandela Washington Fellowship Program for Young African Leaders in 2014. Reading the application, I knew I was underage hence I did not qualify, but I applied anyway. In my application, I mentioned the impact I had brought through my leadership journey and the youth projects I participated in. I also pointed out I had plans to create a career guidance platform for young people when I returned back to Tanzania. I was fortunate to be selected among the five hundred youth out of fifty thousand applicants from sub-Saharan Africa that year.

At this point I knew I wanted to work with people imparting

knowledge. I also wanted to be in a leadership position. This meant taking a career turn. I got a job at Vodacom Tanzania PLC in January 2015 as the manager for training, communications, and incentives. With 6 years in Vodacom, I have taken a couple of career turns as I embraced new roles in quality assurance, financial technology, working in M-Pesa mobile money services, digital care, and automation. I am now leading technical teams even though I did not start out with a technical background. I have been privileged to be coached and mentored by amazing leaders who have helped me on my journey, navigating through my mistakes and triumphs. People who merely saw 'something' in me; always ready to learn and try new things despite being scared.

I've also had friends along my journey who have played vital roles in who I am today. They have been my companions and friends, giving me a shoulder to cry on. They have been my greatest critiques and cheerleaders; holding my hand or simply offering an ear to listen. They have formed part of my support system ensuring I realise my potential, learn from mistakes, and live life to the fullest. They believed in me in the times I doubted myself.

Looking back, I have been shaped by my experiences from home, coaches, mentors, and amazing friends. Resilience, courage, and getting things done together are traits I have seen consistently from my parents and siblings. These have shaped me and contributed greatly to who I am today.

## GOING AGAINST THE GRAIN

I was 16 years old. It was a Tuesday afternoon when my dad took me for my high school application at St. Joseph's Ngarenaro Secondary School. It was a catholic girls school located in Arusha where we lived. I remember being tense during the ride thinking about the interview that would define the future of my education and the agreement I had made with my dad the previous day, while in my mind knowing it was not what I truly wanted. At the gate we were received by a humble gatekeeper, who showed us the way to the reception.

Dad greeted the receptionist with a big smile and said proudly, 'I have brought my daughter for the high school interview. She is one of my last born twins.' We were advised to wait for the headmistress and shown to sit at the long wooden bench outside her office.

After about 10 minutes I was called to a room and given an application form to complete. I had seen this form before, in fact, I had filled it out just yesterday with my dad. He wanted to ensure I would complete it correctly the following day at the school. Going through the details of the form we agreed I was going to study History, Geography, and English Language as my major studies. Dad emphasised how taking those subjects would increase my chances of getting into university in the next two years.

Deep down I knew I did not want to study Geography though I was okay with History and English language. My other option was to take history and two language studies English and Kiswahili, our national language. In my heart, I believed in passing language studies rather than the study of rocks, climate change, and its relation to the people. I loved and enjoyed speaking. I can't remember missing a debate or an opportunity to make a presentation in front of an audience. It came so naturally to me. I had to make a choice, right then. I went with what I believed in while being afraid to my bones of what my dad would do when he realised I had gone against what he had advised me to do. I wrote that I wanted to study History and Language studies English and Kiswahili. Was this going against the grain or simply rebelling? I believed the choice was good for me. It was what I had to do despite what my dad wanted for me. This belief has shaped the many choices I have made for my life. In some instances, it has inspired others to follow their dreams too because they saw I followed mine.

## OBSTACLES AND CHALLENGES ARE PART OF SUCCESS

Three years after working in the East African Community Secretariat, I resigned. This came as a shock to my boss, friends, and family because I was happy with my job, and in fact, I was doing very well. 'Are you sure you want to leave?' asked my boss. 'Is there something wrong?' I replied that nothing was wrong. 'I want to grow and use the lessons I have learned from you and working here.' I told him I believed I could do more with my life and I wanted to lead others. My boss was sad to let me go, but he mentioned he believed that I had something special along with the right attitude so I would thrive anywhere I went. He then accepted my letter. My colleagues in the Public Relations Department encouraged me to go out and explore the world. I was still young and had potential. I left the office feeling I could conquer the world.

I met my friends for coffee to give them my good news. My friends, however, did not see anything good about it. I am not sure if it's because they did not believe I could make a career U-turn and do something different or that I was crazy to leave a job at an international organisation that gave me an opportunity to travel across countries and paid me in US dollars. Or maybe it was that I was moving to the coastal region and they would miss their amazing friend. I guess I will never know. It was my choice to make, wasn't it? Why did their reaction make me feel otherwise? For a moment I doubted if I had made the right choice. What if I left my job and failed where I was going? What did I know about the telecommunications industry? Does having a mobile phone count? What did I know about training others? I was not even certified in training. Would the few youth conferences I had facilitated and trained at count? Was that enough preparation? Was it the same as training people in a corporate environment? I suddenly felt unprepared. I went home crying and asking myself questions; the key one was whether I should go back and retract my resignation letter. I cried some more when I went to bed, and the following week I kept to myself.

I took time to reflect on my strengths and why I applied for a new job. I asked myself, why they had offered me the job. I must have made an impression and shown I could do it. I spoke to my mentor, who was the one who had shared the job advert with me. I told him how I doubted if I was prepared for the new job following what my friends had said. 'What should I do?' I asked him. He told me, 'There is only one way to find out Belinda. Move forward and do the job, give it your best and see. That way you will truly know if you can do it or not.' I went for the job, and 6 years later I am still thriving, learning, and taking many different turns.

Today when I face challenges and obstacles I still cry, albeit a little less than before. There are tears here and there, but they help me relieve the emotions. I don't easily despair as I mostly make a plan, ask for help, and have a positive mindset towards the choices I make. I believe if I don't succeed, I will, at least, learn.

## PLAYING MY PART... BECAUSE IT MATTERS

I have always aspired to assist youth as they journey through life. I hoped that sharing my story and using my experience acquired so far will instigate change, encourage and support others to follow their path, even if it means going against the grain. I am young as

I write this, and in no way have I figured everything out yet, but I am using the resources and ability I have as I keep learning and developing in the process. I believe in limitless possibilities and that we all deserve, and have the power, to lead the life we want for ourselves. I like that it is unique too; a different life.

I founded BORA International with a partner, Helen-Lukundo Chonjo, and together we are on a mission to leverage transformative knowledge, skills, as well as connections for youth advancement.  Through our work, we aim to offer support to Africa's youth, igniting growth within themselves and in their communities. By doing that, we envision a generation of youth who are disrupters, high performing, and transforming their societies.

Having received so much from others, I feel a deep need to 'pay it forward'. I take opportunities to mentor fellow youth and teens as they navigate through school, having career choices to make. I mentor youth as they start their businesses, offering soft skills and leadership training for them to grow sustainably and eventually thrive. I take part in events, competitions, hackathons, grant applications, and business accelerator programs in different capacities as a coordinator, coach, mentor, moderator, speaker, judge, or advisor. This way I am using the skills I have to pay it forward.

I ascribe to the French proverb, 'bloom where you are planted'. At Vodacom where I am currently employed, I take every opportunity to learn from colleagues, peers, subordinates, cleaners and security guards; literary everyone regardless of where they come from. Investing in relationships, I have come to better understand the Saturday's mama made us take care of our home, each one of us playing a different role.

Fifteen months after starting my job in Vodacom Tanzania PLC, my then-line manager resigned. I was a new manager in a new field, however that did not stop me from asking our Director to act in my boss's position as they recruited someone new. I was offered to act as head of the Quality Assurance department for 8 months. I was now managing my fellow managers. It was an important learning opportunity and my peer managers at the quality assurance departments really supported me during this period.

## DARING TO BE ME

When I was in primary school, one of my favourite subjects was Music. I did not only love to sing and learn how to read and write music notations, but also enjoyed the lyrics or the meaning of the songs we were taught. 'It could be a wonderful world' by Pete Seeger was a song that spoke to me about the inequalities that were present in the world back then and I can see them prevailing through the years to today. I aspire to see a better world; one where people are kind to each other, empathetic, and accommodating each other, understanding that our differences are our strengths. A world where skin colour or gender, is not a factor in the opportunities that are presented to us. Through this aspiration I take my kindness, empathy and use my voice and resources to help others. The advancement in technology and communication today makes it easier and more affordable for people to connect across the globe. We should take these opportunities and use the resources we have to create a wonderful world. A world that is better than the one we found. I have made connections with fellow youth across Africa and the world at large to run hackathons that aim to solve challenges in our communities. This way I am doing my part.

I aspire to see more women in senior leadership positions. I commend the efforts done globally today to empower women to take more leadership positions. I am happy to be alive in such a time where government laws are changing to allow women to take part in country leadership, where company policies are updated to include women and their needs in a working environment. There are special programs and emphasis on women's training, coaching and mentorship for their development. I am a beneficiary of numerous programs that have helped me journey my career with a little more courage to go for things I want or believe in, even when I did not have all the requirements and qualifications. I was able to trust in my ability to learn, which became my superpower when I could not check all the boxes. I use the knowledge I acquired to share with women around me, those that I lead, and through the different community programs I run or take part in.

As the leaders of our future, I believe the youth of today should be given opportunities to take part in discussions and activities for our global development. They should be encouraged to do things differently. We all need to do our part in nurturing and preparing future generations. Through BORA International I am imparting youth with knowledge, skills and connections for their advancement, trusting that as they advance they will transform their communities. Through our programs we have seen youth understand themselves better, make bold career choices and seek accountability. They have pursued employment, entrepreneurship, and sometimes both.

I would like to see the future generation embrace being their true self; resisting the urge to be like someone else, or conform to societal expectations. It takes boldness to follow your dreams. As I follow my dreams, I dare you to follow yours. I dare you to just try and see how you will surprise yourself and the world. Dare to be different, dare to be you!

# BELINDA WERA

Belinda is a people, technology, and service enthusiast.

She has an extensive 10-year career working with key players in technology and communication such as Mobile Money, and intergovernmental organizations in Tanzania, East Africa, working across business in areas such as customer experience, mobile money, training, quality assurance, digital transformation, and process automation

Belinda's qualifications are extensive and include a Degree in Public Relations and Marketing from St. Augustine University of Tanzania, a postgraduate Diploma in Business Administration from Wits University, South Africa, and a Masters in Business Administration (MBA) from The Eastern and Southern African Management Institute (ESAMI). Belinda is an Alumni of AIESEC, and President Obama's, Mandela Washington Fellowship 2014.

As an active learner, she always finds ways to teach or share knowledge. Belinda is able to translate complex data into useful insight. Her ability to build and manage relationships enables her to work cross-functionally for the sustainable development of people, processes, systems, and products.

Her mission is to uplift and serve people, organizations, and communities. Her passion for people development has led her to groom leaders in the teams she has led.

As co-founder of BORA International, her commitment continues to provide transformative knowledge, skills, and connections for youth advancement. This is why Belinda has joined Cathy Dimarchos and Solutions2You in the Raise the Baseline Project.

Linkedin:https://www.linkedin.com/in/belinda-wera-40540727/
Email: werab@borainternational.co.tz
Website: www.borainternational.co.tz
Facebook: https://web.facebook.com/belz.jubilant
Instagram: @belztz

# TOP TAKEAWAYS

- Take all the chances and opportunities you can afford. In time you will acquire knowledge, most importantly what works for you and what doesn't.

- Be open to learning and embrace different ways to learn, be it from people, classroom situations, online, wins, failures and mistakes. As you learn, also appreciate the work done by your predecessors.

- Build the criticism and rejection muscle – you need it to grow. Don't hide your work, do what you can and ask for second opinions. People will always give you their opinions whether you ask or not. I believe when you ask, at least you are prepared to receive feedback

- Ask for exactly what you want, the least you can get is a no – you will not die.

- Rest is important for growth. I have come to realise there is power in being able to truly rest in this fast-paced world where one is expected to always be doing something. Rest is essential for survival.

# WHEN THE GRAIN GOES AGAINST YOU

*Catherine Molloy*

W hen someone is going against the grain, it means that they are doing the exact opposite of what would normally be done. They are not doing what's expected of them.

Life began for me in Australia in a children's hospital in Brisbane, where I was left by a mum from a different country. My life was against the grain.

And then, after 8 weeks, I was adopted by 2 gorgeous people, Reg and Helen, my beautiful parents. They definitely went with the grain. They had lovely morals, expectations, knew how to fit into society and made their life their own. Quite a humble existence.

My dad planted over a million seedlings in his life. He bred frogs, and he would have been somebody who could have left the normal routine and been happy living off the land. Yet if you went back a century or 2, that was exactly what everyone did. Whereas in today's society, leaving the rat race to go and be self-sufficient is going against the grain.

So, you know, it's quite an interesting terminology to think about, and also to write about. And I really believe I started life with life going against the grain.

By the age of 7, I had a great group of friends in our neighbourhood and they used to come over to my place. I'd sit there and take down the top 10 songs from the music show Countdown, which was on a Sunday night, then everyone would learn the songs in order for the week. In my room I had little green felt boards and we'd go riding on our bikes, the road-runner gang, until the street lights came on, and we would all scurry home for dinner and homework.

I guess, as a child, I may have gone against the 'normal' grain. I was always thinking a little bit differently, acting a little bit differently. And you can imagine, being adopted, I was different to my parents – they were more reserved, quieter, softer people.

I was a little bit loud and boisterous, always thinking of the next thing to do. Never a dull moment.

So, even growing up in the house I was in, I was definitely against the grain of normality, however, I was lucky because I learned to be kind, I learned to be generous and I learned to be loving – because I was loved.

I think one of the most important things in life I've discovered, whether you're going against the grain or whether you're going *with* the grain, is that love is the most important thing, and we'll talk about that later.

**My life may not have begun as 'normal'** as most people's, however, there was a lot of normality within it. Even people I knew would say they were sorry I was adopted. It truly did not matter to me. My mum told me that when I was 18, I could find my adopted parents – she would help me look. Imagine that! I was very lucky. I was very happy and I was loved and my parents always told me I was wanted, so I grew up very happy that way. **I started to raise funds for the children's hospital about the ripe age of 9.**

My dad was always reading the paper.

I asked him, 'Why are these people's names are in the paper?' He said, 'Because they raise funds or they've done this or that,' so I must have decided at age of 9 I wanted to see my name in print.

What I decided to do, then and there, was to raise money, so I set out to find a good cause. It's interesting that whatever we do in life, even when it's helping others, we have chosen to do it for a reason. It serves a purpose in our life; it might even make us feel good.

Maybe we want to make others feel good. Maybe we don't want others to suffer as we have.

But there's a reason we all do the things we do, and it's not to say, 'Oh gee. Look, my life has purpose because I'm raising money.' There are different reasons for everyone when they choose their causes. But at 9 years old, I chose the children's hospital. I can't really remember why, but when I look back, it's ironic as I started life in the children's hospital. So, I would raise $50 and if I didn't make my $50 through a puppet show I put on, I would walk the streets until I collected the right amount of money. We would send it off, and twice a year, I would run puppet shows in our courtyard and mum would sell homemade lemonade for 5c, and dad would make homemade doughnuts from an antique doughnut maker. They were insanely good.

So, that's some of the little things I did growing up that was against the grain. I did not know of any other child my age who were raising funds for a cause. It's interesting when you start to look back on your life and realise every time there was a read-a-thon or spell-a-thon raising funds for a cause, I would always raise the most money. That's almost a bit ridiculous but I'd end up getting a pile of books with certificates for the Spell-a-thon, the Walk-a-thon – and every other kind of 'thon'! I don't know if you loved walking laps around an oval as much as me, but for me, it meant I was doing something real with my time.

There's an old saying that 'givers gain'. Maybe that was something I learned at a very young age. So what I gained was a great feeling of self-satisfaction and I was able to raise money and help someone else. No doubt I went into the paper, but I can't remember that being a highlight for me – it was the fact that I did it.

When I was raising funds for school, even though we received a book and, some of my favourite stories were from these fundraising books, it wasn't about getting the book, it was that we were able to raise money to help others. I also learnt that time equals money, and both quantities are as precious as each other.

**As a young person, I started to see reward for effort,** and if that effort helped someone less fortunate than me, then I was extraordinarily happy.

One of my top strengths is strategy. I don't know if you know your top 5 strengths but it is certainly worth investing to find out and make sure you are using them well. Maybe I've always had that as a natural strength. 'If I want this end result, what do I need to do to get there?' And I guess that's always been a focus of mine. Perhaps this strength helped me to go against the grain.

I remember when I was in year 6. The year 7 girls pushed a year 5 girl down the stairs. And I was at the bottom of the stairs. I picked her up, looked up at them, and said, 'I'll walk you home. Tell me where you live.'

Every afternoon for the rest of the year, I would meet this girl, and walk her home so she wouldn't get picked on.

And the interesting thing was that she did have a noticeable condition that made her seem a little different to others. She was lovely, she loved life, and had lovely parents. You know in life, we all want the same thing. We want to eat, we want to play, we want to have shelter, we want to have clothes, we want to have fun and we want to be loved. Life is really about gaining pleasure, and for most of us, that means avoiding pain. We don't want to be involved in the pain side of things.

There's not many people who would put themselves out there to be bullied by others from a higher grade to help someone in a lower grade, but that was me.

**At school, most people don't want to go against the grain** and be that person. However, *it was me*, and I have spent my life championing people causes, even before I knew of Mother Teresa, and before I went to her house in Kolkata and read the sign. 'If you can't feed 100 – feed one.'

That was something I truly believed in and have had many lessons along the way.

**Quite often, it only takes only one person to stand up and stand out, to make that difference.**

I hope reading this chapter may help you feel like you are someone who can make a difference too.

When I moved into high school, I would like to say I went against the grain there too, but I don't feel I did.

I tend to think ... we moved more as a pack. But I never did anything that I thought would hurt someone else.

Until year 9, I was standing in a tuckshop line, one girl turned to another, picking on her, and said, 'I'll have you in the alley this afternoon.'

Now, this girl was younger, she was smaller, she was in tears – this was the bully of the school.

I said, 'I don't think you should have her. Why don't you pick on someone your own size?' Once again my big mouth was going to get me in trouble – going against the grain of staying quiet and staying out of things.

By this stage, half the school knew there was going to be a fight that afternoon, as Sally went around telling everyone. So many people turned up.

My cousin was there, 3 grades higher, asking me, 'What are you doing? She's the school bully,'

I said, 'I don't know, but she was picking on a younger, smaller person, and I thought she should be picking on someone her own size.'

**So, going against the grain does sometimes get you into trouble.**

But you know what, it's the passionate people who make a difference.

So, I am ashamed of what happened that day, and I've never spoken about it in any of my stories, ever.

But she had her hands up saying, 'Come on, hit me.' And I said, 'No. You picked this fight so you hit me.' Everyone was standing and cheering, 'Fight. Fight. Fight.' I don't know if you've ever put yourself in a situation that you wished you didn't, but I was in one that day.

This went on for a little bit, and everyone was starting to yell out. I just wanted it over and done with. That was my one big wrong decision.

When I realized she didn't want to hit me I should have walked away.

I had a fear she may have come from behind, and I also felt she may continue to bully me as a coward.

So I threw a punch. I had an older brother and we used to wrestle all the time. I was always blocking and ducking and weaving.

I loved to watch Haystack Calhoun, the wrestler with the

horseshoe around his neck. We used to watch Muhammad Ali, who fights like a butterfly and stings like a bee.

I was a fast runner, athletic, good on my feet. I'm sorry, I just quickly threw one punch.

She raised her hand. She had a watch on and the watch punched back into her nose and the metal button scratched it.

I said, 'I'm really sorry,' as blood came out, and then she went home. I went home. It was not a nice experience and I would never ever, ever say for anyone to do that. Hands are made for loving each other; for healing not hurting. My parents never hit us with their hands and I never hit my children with my hands either.

The one good outcome from this was she never picked another fight with anyone again.

The second outcome was people were then looking up to me but it was for all the wrong reasons.

*

Sometimes when we stand up for others, when we're passionate, we don't always understand the domino effect. And I don't think that we should hold back from standing up for others, but I also feel we should never ever touch another human being. That was a first in my life.

And I do hope I never have to physically defend myself ever again.

The reason I'm sharing this story now, is because I've always gone against the grain to stand up for what I think is right. Humans are my weakness and maybe that was why I was made a Global Goodwill Ambassador later in life for the work we do.

**By doing what we think is right, wrong things can sometimes happen.**

But I also don't want to deter you from not standing up for

what you believe in.

Just sometimes when we reflect, we understand there are different ways of doing things.

But what this allowed me to do was then spread more kindness, more generosity, within the school, and I can't remember anyone ever picking fights with people after that.

So something good came out of it, as well as the bad, which I had to live with.

By the time I turned 16, my mum passed away very suddenly.

It will always bring tears to my eyes. Whenever I've needed help I think, 'What would Mum do?' She was just love.

She had just started stepping into her own.

Mum was making pottery. She won every category at the exhibition from wheel throne to handmade to cutting sculptures. She was very talented. I love how we can't do everything in one season but there is a season for everything. No matter what stage we're at in life, or where we're at, it's never too late to try something new or do what we love. Life can change in an instant.

**Don't let yesterday use up today.** Make decisions and step into your heart's desire. Mum showed me how from a hobby she created a business, won awards and was sought after. Little quiet mum who always sacrificed for us, bought her first car herself – a royal blue Statesman with white leather interior and electric windows.

**If we don't disrupt ourselves at times, then we will be disrupted.**

Here we are in 2021, a new decade with a big disruption. Yet they say every 100 years we have a health crises – still we weren't ready for it. Governments hadn't planned for it. They were advised in November 2019.

COVID-19 has pushed people in many directions.

We don't have a looking glass. We can't tell 10 years from

now what the outcome will be from the actions we've taken, but 'no action' never leads to the best action.

By my late teens, I had 3 jobs – I worked in the bank, I worked night-shift, I worked doing aerobics and silver service waitressing and I was saving money to be able to have short trips overseas to third world countries that were giving me good bang for my buck, as well as the most amazing experiences. I started studying body language and this was a tipping point for my future.

I think that was one of the key turning points in my life; understanding people, understanding just through a hand shake, who that person is – whether they're soft, whether they're gentle, whether they're firm and decisive, whether they're eager to meet you or cautious. This all came through very quickly from the touch. It taught me so much and then, understanding and reading body language, not just to read others as body language is very subjective, but for me to understand my body language and how it was affecting conversations. That's what I teach today.

So even as a young person, I very quickly started topping sales in the bank. I moved into the training area, delivering customer service and product knowledge.

And, of course, I used body language to make those big differences, to provide the best service and to hit those sales.

I loved my job, and I wasn't going to leave my job.

I met my husband, and I said to him at the time that he might not want to marry me because I didn't want to have children. He was 7 years older than me and told me he couldn't have children. I said, 'Fantastic – a marriage made in heaven.'

In actual fact, we then had 3 children in 3 years.

When I was pregnant with my first one it was definitely meant to be.

I mean, going back to those days, everyone had children. So

once again, for me to decide not to have children really was going against the grain.

**But sometimes, the universe has other plans for us** and it may feel like the grain will go against us.

But it was definitely for the best.

And I think every time the grain goes against us, that is a great time to stop and reflect to see the gift that has been given and needs to be unwrapped.

Even if someone dies early, the gift is still there, lessons are still learnt, even bad experiences teach us what not to do and what to do.

I gave birth to 2 boys and a girl and they were absolutely amazing. We'd have pyjama days, beach days, picnic days, park days … and I still cherish those moments today.

I was very lucky I was able to create and run 3 businesses from home to help support the children. I had a clothes business, a book business, and a toy business; absolutely perfect for children.

I also got to meet many beautiful mothers, who I am still friends with today.

I was always very adaptable, flexible, creative, and influential. I think that has been what's got me through life. I've learnt to adopt many skills and tools, and make them work for me.

Unfortunately, during my third pregnancy my father fell ill, and by the time he went to the doctor he had cancer throughout his body and in his bones. They gave him 3 months to live, and he lived for a year, which was an amazing time to share with him.

However, it was hard. I ended up with 4 autoimmune diseases, and I remember the doctor asking me how I managed to get up in the mornings. I said, 'I just take one leg out of bed, then I get the other leg out, and then I'm up.'

**I wasn't going to wallow in these issues.** I had made the decision I was going to be okay. Going against doctor's orders, I soldiered on.

It was a struggle to balance everything and I was probably running on empty at times. However, I loved being a mum, a wife and a friend, and was grateful for pulling through.

In 2008, in the GFC (the global financial crisis that we apparently didn't have in Australia!), my husband fell ill. I had to leave my children at home and run my husband's business.

I loved it. It was real estate. I ended up selling 5 houses in one week, 3 in a day, and it was a record for the 20 year old business. I told my husband I wanted to keep his business running but he didn't think he would get better while we still had the business.

So we decided to sell a business in the middle of the GFC, with all the properties tied to it.

That was that.

**We lost over a million dollars.** We were left with a mortgage on a house and 3 children in school, with no jobs or money coming in. I quickly took action before the banks caught up with the facts. I decided to get back into education and training – that's what I love and everyone needs; customer service.

So I started a training company using some mortgage money and was quickly ready to deliver customer service training again but then we discovered people wanted leadership and management training, even though today, thank goodness, people are realising how important good customer service is too.

So I told my husband I was going to start a business, not having been in the workforce for about 15 years.

**Sometimes what you don't know is a good thing** – you don't know what you don't know.

If someone had told me I was going to work 7 days a week for, say, 10 years, and then, another crises would cross my path and take it all away again, would I have done it? Truthfully, probably not. But it was definitely an amazing heartfelt journey. When I started the business I decided I would give 10% of profits to charity. My husband couldn't understand it, as we'd just lost so much money. But I wanted to be working towards something bigger than just us. For me, there's always something bigger.

For those of you haven't travelled and now can't travel, it's easy to get caught up in our little world.

But when you are a traveller, and you've seen so much and met so many people, and live in so many different cultures, you realize we are all one. We all have the same foundational needs as humans.

**Some people have the basics and some don't.**

For me, globally helping people is not a problem – it's something I need to do.

I also gave time fundraising for our local communities; P&F tuckshop duties, soccer coaching, Sunday school teaching, raising money for riding with the disabled, being on the board of Red Cross and helping the homeless.

There are so many wonderful things we can do and bring our joy to. Through my business we've created teenager programs to be able to give them strong mental wealth and purpose for the future.

I truly have found when you are working towards goals or a bigger purpose than just you, life is better, life has meaning. Sometimes we may feel like we are swimming upstream, but everything will unfold, and then you will complete the circle of life. I find there is not just one circle, but many.

As a child, after the words 'mum' and 'dad', my next word was 'horse' – I loved them. I would stand beside a pony at a fete and my parents would pick me up 2 hours later. In my room as a teenager, my bedspread and posters were horses. Finally, I owned my own on Valentine's day when I was 16 and I called him St. Valentine. I have no idea what his real name was, and he was stamped with a heart.

Now at 55, I own a horse again and ride on the weekends. When I was 7 I used to teach my peers, and then at the age of 42, I started training peers again in business through to CEOs and Fortune 500 companies. There are many circles that happen in our life; from raising funds for children at the age of 9, to spending the last 12 years raising funds for orphans around the world – another full circle. Taking my business global in 2014 and travelling the world again – travel happened to be one of my favourite things to do in my late teens and early 20's – full circles.

**What full circles are you creating?** What did you love to do as a child that you are still doing today?

One of the most important things I did through times of crisis was to learn. I did my Masters in Neuro-Linguistic Programming. I did diplomas and degrees in business and leadership management. I upgraded my coaching skills.

One thing I would suggest is – everyone keeps learning. They say, if you think you know everything, you may as well die! Stay curious not furious in life.

Keep learning, because when you learn, you can share and implement some of the tools you've learned and make a difference in someone's life.

**One of the big things I've learned is that what we think isn't always right.** Just because we think something doesn't mean it's true.

We all say things, but our behaviour shows us who we really are.

Fundraising was consuming me when I was running my

company, so I wrote a book called, *The Million Dollar Handshake*. What a difference that made! One-third of the profits go to Watoto and orphans in Africa. With my other book, *The Conscious Leader,* one-third of profits go to children dying of cancer in India. We are supporting doctors to help care for these children over a 12 month period. We can make a difference and by changing our thought process we can change our actions.

Swimming upstream at times has been hard, but worth it. I would like to be more controversial than I am and, maybe one day soon, I will be ready to go against the grain again and speak out globally for what I stand for. But right now, I will continue to support the people who cannot support themselves, and write programs and educational documents to help people who are ready to make a difference, champion children and give them rights to education and creativity, and stand up for those who are not being heard.

**Your legacy is your true currency.** What are you consciously transferring to someone else? What do you want to be known for? In 2009 we lost our business and properties. I started a business to keep our children at school and in the family home, as well as to raise funds for our local community.

By 2010 my business had sold over a million dollars in training and education and I was donating time on Thursdays to a program called 'Shine', for children who need love and friendship. Here I heard about orphans in Watoto and the needs of the people there. I joined the fund raising committee on the Sunshine Coast. In 2012, I went to Uganda to help build homes and took my 15-year-old daughter with me. In 2014, I was appointed to the local council education taskforce, and went to China to speak. I built connections we still do business with today. My business grew. I spoke in Saudi Arabia, Dubai, UK, India, Hong Kong,

Singapore, just to name a few, and hundreds of cities around the world. I won awards in education and training in America and an Asia pacific award for our Conscious Connection Framework. I was made a Global Goodwill Ambassador for the work I do as a humanitarian. 30% of profits were being donated to charity.

Then the COVID-19 crises hit; another major global crises only 10 years on from the last one. I flew out of Egypt in March 2020 after speaking to 750 women. Our live events, as we knew them, closed down around the world. We could not make it back to Africa to build lives and homes; we could only work from afar. We have learnt to share powerful messages from our home stages for virtual influence. Life will continue to change and evolve. We must to.

I have taken this time to finish my Masters in Leadership, write my book *The Conscious Leader* and share messages of hope, and how to build mental wealth. When we have hope and give hope there is always a better future. When we are conscious of our footprint on this planet, we are the difference. What is the gift in the present moment for you to unwrap? It may be too early to reflect yet ... but soon.

**Personal power comes from consciously using the right emotion at the right time** ... go against the grain – keep pushing, and understand there is a season for everything you want to do. Sometimes we can't have it all in the one season. My season of motherhood was amazing. My season of building business was extraordinary. My season of being a philanthropist gave me hope. My season of COVID-19 gave me loss, but has given me time.

So here I am again in life, going against the grain. Or is the grain going against me? Either way I accept the challenge to continue making a difference on this beautiful planet we've been gifted and, through education and love, let's hope the human spirit can change from people thinking of themselves first, to rather them having good intentions for the people they meet. No more hurting someone else to pleasure ourselves, no more hurting someone else to make ourselves feel better, no more hurting the planet or animals.

**Go against the grain and be the hero in someone else's journey.**

# CATHERINE MOLLOY

Fun, friendly and forward thinking, Communication Expert Catherine Molloy reveals the hidden psychology behind connection and influence and provides people with the keys to revolutionise their communication effectiveness.

With over 30 years' experience in business, education, speaking and transforming lives all over the world, she believes that business success rests on the ability to build real connections at velocity. Catherine Molloy is a communication expert specialising in sales service and leadership and has spoken in over 150 cities world wide as a corporate and inspirational speaker and facilitator. She is the famous author of The Business Book of the Year by Orion books, *The Million Dollar Handshake*. This book has been translated into many different languages all around the world.

Catherine's new book *The Conscious Leader* was released in 2021 and is already an amazon best seller. Catherine has been made a Global Goodwill Ambassador for her tireless work in supporting abandoned women and children and has been travelling to Uganda since 2010 to help build homes for orphans and vulnerable women and create education programs called 'unlock your worth'. She also supports the BOMBAY mothers and children's hospital in Mumbai, India and local charities in Australia

Her thought leadership is in how to hack the psychology of communication to build lasting connections, fast. Catherine has owned and operated several highly successful training companies and been recognised both nationally and internationally as a leader in sales and service training. As CEO and Founder of Auspac Business Advantage, she was recently awarded an International "Stevie Award" in America for Sales Training/Education Leader of the Year, and received the Australian Institute of leadership and management award. After training internationally, Catherine has developed the Conscious Connection Framework. It is a holistic roadmap that combines insights from over 30 years of studying body language, leadership, behavioural science and Neuro-Linguistic Programming to radically transform how teams and individuals self-lead and communicate. Catherine uses a variety of different tools to help build confidence, courage and grow your business. These skills have been honed during her extensive experience teaching cross-culturally and her passion to help people succeed. Join Catherine's interactive keynotes and trainings where you can make real changes during these sessions to create more positive outcomes for yourself and your business. This desire to build multicultural relationships and cultivate health communication skills also features outside of work. Catherine is a humanitarian, lives on a sustainable farm with her family, she travels from Brisbane, Australia and loves working with all cultures of the world.

Connect with Catherine at  www.catherinemolloy.com.au
https://www.linkedin.com/in/catherinemolloy/

# TOP TAKEAWAYS

- Love unconditionally – no one owes you anything – when you do things do them from the heart and don't expect anything in return. If you don't want to do something don't. Don't do it and then whinge about it and try to mater yourself. Just do it with love!

- Kindness is not weakness – if you cant help 100 help one … everyone matters, your smile makes a difference in this world. You will never be replaced on this planet and neither will the person beside you or the person beside them, no one is more important than another, so lets help each other and stay kind.

- There is a season for everything – when you believe in yourself others believe in you too. When you believe in yourself you can face the seasons of life as they occur. God has given us many gifts and we are challenged to use them at times.

Don't forget to stay doing the things that gave you most joy as a child, you will see many circles in life and acknowledge them when they occur and be grateful for them. There is a present in every crises to be unwrapped and used again. Your presence in the present, matters to the world.

# THINK BIG, THINK LIMITLESSLY

*Cathy Dimarchos*

**D**oubt, hesitation or even fear are our initial responses, our instinct, when it comes to THINKING BIG, THINKING LIMITLESSLY and GOING AGAINST THE GRAIN. It is our built-in mechanism to keep us safe, especially when we are told to 'stay in our lane' and that 'it does not work that way.' As a child, it's normal behaviour to explore, to take risks and push boundaries. So how is it we get to adulthood and come to a grinding halt? Why is it that going against the grain becomes taboo?

When I look back to my childhood, I recognise that I was not your typical first-generation immigrant. I played football and cricket with the boys on the streets, climbed trees, rode a skateboard and even gave surfing a crack. As I developed from a young child to a teenager, those suggestions of who I was and whom I was meant to be encroached on what I was doing, preventing me in many ways of 'being me'.

*Was I giving power away to others? Was I letting my parents down if I did not conform?*

Part of our journey in life is to please others, especially those that we love and respect, so we change our lens from what we want to do to what we feel we 'should' be doing, based on what we see others do and what we are told is the 'right' thing to do.

That dichotomy in my head of what I needed to do versus what I wanted to do became a constant, but I always remember that my parents' voices (especially my father's), encouraged 'choice'. It was about me being aware and conscious of the choices I made. Theirs' was the voice of reason and logic from a perspective of a 'lived' life – one filled with many challenges, but nonetheless, a subjective one that I valued.

What a privilege I had to be given choices and 'shown' there was value in people, more so than anything else in life.

I was not a loud person and somewhat shy – I still am. But if I was to reflect on my earlier years, I recognise that others may have seen me as confident and strong. This was a far cry from how I felt often feeling I didn't fit in. I would play it safe by keeping busy, not picking sides, and being mindful of others' choices.

Conscious choices and values underpinned my actions. Don't get me wrong, I made mistakes, but they became lessons; ones that are still vivid by image and emotion.

Like most families, there were arguments and conflicts, but even in those moments, I was able to see things through multiple lenses. I had the privilege of being raised by my grandmother who had a different perspective on life. The family disagreements caused rifts and scars, which over time would heal, but the process allowed me to become more conscious of my personal perspective, words and actions. Wounds heal over time, and through these experiences, I came to understand that what may work for me, might not work for someone else. There is no 'one right way'. Judgment of self is far stronger than judgment from others. We only need to look at sporting events to see the impact on athletes as they self-reflect on their performance when they feel they could have done more. Nothing can be stronger than the punishment they place on themselves for missing an opportunity or not performing at their peak.

When I reflect on 'going against the grain' and what it truly means to me, it is so much more than doing things differently. It's about identifying and accepting differences and change, with the ability to stand back, reflect and breathe. It allows us to observe the lens we are using and then to make a choice to see the moment through a different lens. The initial feeling of fear, doubt and perhaps rejection, is something I relate to and recognise has held me back at times. When I look at it now, I can acknowledge that 'first order thinking' is what forms a lot of what we all do. Most of us act upon the first reaction we have. This is driven by what we have seen occur in the past and perhaps still see now, so we accept it is the norm. It is no surprise that we then act in the same way we have always acted.

I, like most people, was raised to listen in a way that I could potentially hear what was going to be asked of me. As an example, in the classroom, the teacher speaks and provides us with content. We listen so that if we are asked a question we can instantly put up our hand to show we have been attentive. But over time, I began to realise that what we hear is often *not* what is being said. These little lessons began with my grandmother. I would hear her interpretation of a series of events, whilst also hearing different versions from others in the family. I quickly realised people held several different perspectives. Being quite young, my view seldom mattered so I never found the need to share my voice, but this also established a pattern – in hearing, seeing and seldom speaking. I would pause, stand back and reflect, but seldom get caught up in the debates. I kept busy through sport and other activities and mixed with many different groups, but was never tied to anyone. I was happy and loved the life I lived, as there was a great deal of autonomy. I recall joyous moments with cousins, and some of those memories still bring a huge smile to my face.

I look back and recognise it as a time when I would consider the implication of any situation in any given moment, but then also consider step 2 and step 3. I guess in short, I thought about the risks versus the impact for the short term, and then looked at potential options and solutions in the long term. I'm not sure if this became a pattern from my family experiences or a combination of family and community.

I have vivid memories of a strong feeling of values when playing games with friends in the back lane, so if there were boundaries being crossed, I was able to find my voice. I had a strong sense of wanting to 'do right' by others. This was something I modelled on my father. He often looked out for others and had a drive for justice and equality beyond himself. His desire to help those less fortunate was always seen through his actions and his words. He could be strong-minded but he was gentle when it came to helping and uplifting others.

I look at life now and recognise we live in a faced-paced environment that is forever changing. Sometimes I feel like I'm on a merry-go-round that doesn't stop, and part of this fast pace has me looking to 'fix' things immediately so I can move on to the next thing. I call it 'the chase'. It's about taking an immediate approach, the one that is most obvious, the path everyone else has taken or suggested because I, too, want to belong. I am no different in that way.

## Pausing to better understand

But as I have come to understand who I am and my true purpose in life, I have recognised the value in pausing.

Pausing gives me breath. It allows me to look at the long-term impact, to consider the ripple effect and to ask, 'What else, who else, and how will this one decision today have an impact in years to come?'

I began a journey in 2014, one that was not mine, but one that I would share with my daughter, and it has shaped me to be the person I am today. As I write this book, I recognise I have not reached a destination but am still on a journey of discovery, lessons and forever evolving.

I was shadowing my then 17-year-old daughter, who was on a personal mission. She chose Africa as a place to volunteer when she finished school, and at the time she made her decision, Ebola had broken out.

It was a long way from home and she was so young, so I'm sure you can hear my husband's voice say, 'No, choose somewhere else,' as we sat at the dining table and she announced her decision. My son and I looked at each other, then at her, and back to my husband, holding back for just a moment before we both blurted out, 'WHY?'

Her logic was sound to her – it was where she could have a greater impact!

As a family, we are big believers in 'paying it forward', so why was this any different? As I listened to her, I could not help but think, 'How can this work where everyone feels heard and her vision is not crushed?' There was a solution to be reached, with several strategies needing to be considered.

Her commitment to volunteer for 3 months was driven by passion, determination and perhaps some risk. There was also an element of naivety, but that meant we all needed to work together to find a way forward.

This led to the beginning of the journey I believe has brought me to where I am today. She spent the initial month of her trip alone in Arusha with Projects Abroad, to discover who she was and how she wanted to contribute to the children she worked with at various orphanages.

As I look back at that moment around the dining table where we all had different ideas, I recognise it would have been easier to simply say 'No,' but as I was shown throughout my life, choices when considered and thought-out can lead to opportunities. That moment was about mitigating risk. The initial response we all had was part of our learned behaviours. It was automated, but as we sat back and discussed things over the next few months, it became a process of thinking about every stage, and then, 'What if? What else? Who else?'

Her choice of Africa was *going against the grain,* as some of her friends had contemplated trips to Canada, the USA and Fiji, but she chose to create an impact and go where nobody had gone before, doing it her way.

The day she flew out was another impactful moment for me as I placed my hand on the glass window at the airport, where it met her hand on the other side at customs, as she headed to board the flight. That doubt, hesitation and fear I had reminded me of a previous error in judgment that came flooding back, but by that stage, it was too late. She had gone through customs and was heading to her gate to board the plane.

There is so much more I can share about that moment and the journey we all took to get there, but I share this small part of the story with you because it is important for all of us to be able to have difficult discussions, to accept that we are different, and to walk away feeling heard. Today, I recognise that as a defining moment for me, but it took several months for me to realise it.

I have come to recognise moments where I can better manage a difficult conversation, reflect on those moments and then continue to learn to listen with more care.

The reality is we all, at times, need to step back from our initial reactions, and be prepared to dig deep to observe what it is that we want for ourselves and for those around us. I understand now, that to pursue something bigger than me comes with risk, but having a belief it can be done is a start.

When I joined my daughter one month later, the subsequent two months would be a journey of a lifetime. We experienced life! We volunteered in orphanages, trekked alongside gorillas, spent time with chimpanzees, lived with the Maasai, built a water tank, brought water into an orphanage, dug trenches for a new school, taught English and cried a lot.

We argued and laughed, but most of all we recognised that she was right; we could do so much more where we were, and we could have an impact. She learnt to speak Swahili (no, not me, I relied on her for that), and through her commitment to learn the language, we understood so much more about the children. She spent time questioning, listening and understanding what was in instances, normally difficult to gauge as an outsider.

For me there were many moments of crystallisation. The fact that I consider myself privileged became even more evident as I sat talking with the Maasai and seeing firsthand the vast differences in culture.

### Listening to begin to understand

I recall a distinct moment where we recognised the value in 'listening to begin to understand.' I use the word 'begin' because it is so relevant when we come from such different lived experiences. Being present in those moments meant we needed to leave our 'western views' behind and simply hold the space to listen. We had the honour of hearing stories and perspectives of people who lived with 3 generations of family in a Boma (traditional Maasai home) in remote areas where water and electricity were limited. A place where men have multiple wives and celebrate the expansion of family. There were rituals and customs hundreds, if not thousands, of years old. This incredible culture is so strong it has survived the test of time and threats from modern civilisation. Yet we have crept in and I couldn't help but think we are encroaching, as there were signs that new ways are being embraced by the younger warriors. Once again, the need to simply listen was paramount.

In a strange way, being there felt like home. I cannot explain it, but I had an incredible sense of peace and an ability to sleep soundly, something I've not been able to do for some 25 years. It was a place you could wake up in the morning and see a giraffe standing outside, or late in the afternoon watch zebras run past as Maasai men herded their cattle to bring them in for the night to protect them from the lions. It was not a place you could be outside when the sun set as there were predators roaming, looking for their next meal.

After some 7 years and multiple trips back, some with family and friends, I recognise the power in shared knowledge and lived experiences. I saw that I could contribute at a higher level and pay things forward on a larger scale. This is how Raise the Baseline project was born https://www.solutions2you.com.au/raise-the-baseline.

My last visit to Africa was in 2018. It was tumultuous for me as there was much that would impact me emotionally, and it also led to an urgent flight home, with my mother critically ill in hospital.

## Realigning my values

This was the beginning of a period of realigning my values. Once again, I needed to define my purpose in life, what I truly wanted to do with my time, with whom I would spend it, and what impact I truly want to make.

I loved the work I was doing developing people at grass roots and imparting knowledge to leaders across the world, but there were rumbles, and I began to see misalignment in my core values. By March 2019, it came to grinding halt. My boundaries were crossed and I knew I needed to do more and to be more. When the pandemic hit, I was travelling across the country speaking at events. I flew back from Perth on March 13, 2020 and on March 17 my father had a fall that would leave us devastated. On March 20, my mother was rushed to a different hospital to be treated by a cardiac team, and on March 21 we sadly lost my father.

We had gone into full lockdown and it was amidst all of this that my road forward became clearer. I needed to do more; I needed to be more.

Mum was critical and at risk, so after 24 hours of her blood pressure sitting at 229, I made the decision to discharge her into my care. This meant leaving her home behind and starting a new life with our family.

Crisis brings about clarity and determination, and yes it has its challenges, but again I found myself in a privileged position. My understanding and nurturing husband and children would be there to care for my mum 24 hours a day with me. Mum was not well, and it was months of recovery before she was able to walk and talk to anyone and begin her healing.

This period allowed me to think beyond me and I began to engage online and support young leaders in Tanzania. I found myself drawn back to what felt like my other home, a place I knew I could create an impact. My commitment to doing more and being more was forming, but I had not crystallised the bigger picture. The journey was born with some grit and determination on my part, as well as a willingness and trust from some of the young people I had previously worked with. My trips to Tanzania over the years enabled me to cross paths with some amazing humans. Whilst I had not previously recognised the power of connection, it has led me to where I am now; bringing together the people that form part of this book and the development of the Raising the Baseline project.

The amazing humans in this book have all crossed my path at some stage. When we first met, there was a connection that left an imprint, but most of all, there was an alignment of values. Each person in this book has been courageous to 'go against the grain' leaving an impact, so as you read this book and their stories, I hope you can see the value and magic that occurs when people cross paths and when we take the opportunity to pause and get to know them. When we align in values and are prepared to do things differently, we can bring about change that will shape a better world for our future generations.

As I reflect on my career, I can see now that I did things differently. I know that Business Advisory is more than business, to me it is about people and what they want to achieve for themselves. It's about showing people how they can lead and take others with them on the journey. It's about creating opportunities that show others the personal gain we can achieve with the power in collaboration and by seeing others succeed.

When we can show people they belong and help them to feel supported and valued, no matter where they are across the globe, they will do the same for those around them. The power is in the 'showing' as this creates a ripple effect.

The co-authors of this book are not only sharing their stories with you, they are paying it forward in supporting us with the programs we have developed to inspire and transform young people across the globe. We are starting in Tanzania because it is a place close to my heart. It is the place that has reshaped me and given me a vision of the person I want to become. It is the place that has enabled a stranger to reach out and ask for help with a business plan and an idea. In many ways it is the birthplace of where today's leaders will help to shape a better tomorrow so that future generations can lead the life they deserve.

So, as we bring this book to life and it is held tightly in your hands, you too are contributing to changing the lives of many.

My chapter has just begun. The story of Raise the Baseline will create new stories in your life and in that of those whom we help to develop.

Do I have fear, doubt and hesitation? At times I do, but as I pause to reflect, I recognise this is bigger than me, and that these emotions don't prevent me from taking action. In fact, they drive me to do better, and to search for likeminded people, so that we, as a collective, can contribute and elevate those around us. Together we will create a better tomorrow, one person at a time, and we will show others that they can 'go against the grain' and succeed.

**Going against the Grain is about "standing up and owning your voice"**
To be honest, this has only become evident in the past couple of years when it was suggested that my keynote speaking topic, at the Empowered Women summit be, 'Standing up and owning your voice'. I reflected on what it meant. Initially I drew on an incident very early in my career when it was suggested I go home to change because I was wearing a suit with pants. As you can imagine, I voiced my opinion on that! But as time passed, I began to see patterns in my life, and in my career. I had overlooked them and talked about my experiences as factual events.

When I reflect on my younger years, I believe the power of choice that was instilled in me also became the voice of reason. It enabled me to pause, reflect and then respond, and in that process, I was given permission to do things differently. Whilst in school there were many things that were prescriptive, even to the shade of the colour of our stockings, there was a constant at home of being able to choose and to do things 'my way'.

It may also explain, why I had never considered it to be 'going against the grain' but  simply saw it as the ability to choose.

The message to me means to give others permission to do things their way, and by supporting them, we can create a path that encourages them to keep steering forward. It diminishes the doubt and hesitation that inevitably comes from doing things differently.

My commitment in calling this out is to acknowledge the power that it holds and to ensure that our future generations have the ability, creativity and passion to bring about a change we need to see in the world. It is only likely to occur by doing things differently. It's important they know we will support them, and that through collaboration and acceptance, they will steer forward in ways that may not have been considered before.

This book is about paving the way so they can steer ahead.

**Challenges and obstacles are a way to show us that we can navigate forward differently.**

I am constantly faced with challenges and obstacles and I have not mastered these by any means.

There are a few questions I ask myself in these moments: What is in my control? If I can control the impact or the outcome, I will take on board all that is in front of me. My influence needs to consider 'second order thinking' as I look at the immediate impact in reacting now, and then consider the implications for holding back and planning with consideration. Then I ask, 'What might happen if I react now but what may happen with a different decision?' If I do not have control, I move on.

I am still faced with the initial emotion of fear, but I have begun the process of recognising it and acknowledging it. I always go back to 'pause, listen and listen some more', so I can understand what is really being said, or more likely, what is *not* being said.

We have often heard people sharing their tips on how to respond, and to seek more details going beyond what is presented. With this in mind, I have found that what often appears to be an obstacle, is really about timing, or one small aspect of a bigger picture, and it may not be as challenging as originally thought.

If I could take you back to my daughter sitting at the dining table sharing her vision, this was an obstacle, a challenge. But as I shared earlier, through some confronting discussions and taking the time to allow each person to be heard, we were able to create a path forward that we were all okay with. Yes, there was still resistance and fear but the obstacle was navigated to a point where she could still follow her passion.

**My contribution to the future generation**

I see our future generation holding so many gifts at such a young age – ones that have taken me years to recognise and work on myself. I acknowledge that children as young as 10 can show me how to be a better person, especially when we see them on television shows such as MasterChef competing against one another, yet supporting and genuinely encouraging one another to succeed.

It is in these moments we can pause and take a step back and allow them to showcase themselves as individuals and as part of a team. I would love for us all to take the opportunity to hand over power, encourage them to take risks and make mistakes so that they can keep discovering things about themselves.

In business, we can create opportunities by giving them a chair at the table and asking them to contribute, genuinely allowing them to share their thoughts and showcase themselves as peers. We can be vulnerable and courageous at the same time and make our voices redundant, allowing them to create a future that will work for them.

The future is not a race, so if we take a slow and measured approach that not only fuels us but those around us, we will create a path that encourages, uplifts and bring others on the journey with us. A personal journey may be self-fulfilling but will be left unnoticed if it is alone. A shared journey creates impact and will survive us all.

**What we choose to do today matters. Our future generation's choices today will shape tomorrow**

As the world becomes closer in distance, it also seemingly creates division. Proximity is no longer about personal space, but how we choose to engage and the impact that engagement will make.

My dream and commitment is to bring people together to share in knowledge and uplift one another.

We all have the ability to contribute no matter where we are born or where we are living. Our willingness do so is key. Time, commitment and consistency will create a ripple effect, so as you begin your journey through life in search of your future, consider what else you might be able to do that will impact someone in the world. Consider who you might like to bring on the journey with you and how your contribution to someone's life will bring joy to what you do.

I was recently asked if it was possible for one person to change the world. As I reflected on the magnitude of what was being said, as daunting as it may sound, the reality is that the answer is yes!

All it takes is one person, one belief and one action. Whether we know it or not, a ripple effect occurs through the shared experience of 2 individuals. The act of showing and doing without realising has affected those around them and whilst it may not create a reaction in that moment, it will create a response down the track.

We do not need to see the impact for it to be real, we simply need to believe that by doing, we are creating.

For those reading this book, I want to thank you as you are already contributing to developing a future leader somewhere in the world. I also hope you find what you are looking for on your path forward and that you are inspired by the amazing humans in this book, as they have each contributed to my journey and have inspired me to continue to learn and relentlessly give back.

If you would like to be part of the project please reach out https://www.solutions2you.com.au/raise-the-baseline

Thank you for gifting your time to reading *Going Against the Grain*.

# CATHY DIMARCHOS

Cathy Dimarchos is an award-winning business advisor, mentor, coach, and TEDx and keynote speaker working internationally and locally. She is an indefatigable philanthropist who believes we can all contribute to lifting the baseline of people across the world, one person at a time.

Cathy is the founder of Solutions2You, born from her passion to serve and to leave a lasting imprint by creating paths that enable people to lead the lives they deserve. As a professional advisor and motivational voice, Cathy dedicates her time to perfecting a combination of people, business and situational skills, delivering tangible business toolkits and solutions to clients from every imaginable background.

Working across international borders and cultures highlighted the importance of seeing different perspectives and embracing her professional lives holistically. Her values took centrestage and business became honest and expressive. She believes knowledge exchange leads to effective and sustainable outcomes.

Backed by 35 years in finance, setting up and scaling businesses and counselling qualifications, Cathy says her calling enables her to support people to realise their unspoken ambitions, stepping outside the comfort zones that regularly hold them back. Through empathy and strategic positioning, she empowers people to establish healthy professional boundaries, think limitlessly and challenge norms, while rediscovering a curiosity for knowledge.

Cathy has said her initial trip to East Africa was one of her greatest challenges, but has also proven to be the most rewarding. Her time living with the Maasai, building water tanks, teaching English and working in orphanages and baby crisis centres, enabled her to crystalise her vision of 'paying it forward'. She has made several trips with family and friends since 2014, and is committed to a project she has developed, supporting young leaders and entrepreneurs so they can shape a better tomorrow.

Her advisory services extend to corporates, boards, teams, SMEs and individuals empowering them to become 'anti-fragile' in a world that is forever changing, stretching their boundaries and enabling them to create a psychologically safe environment with a social impact.

Cathy facilitates programs for change-makers, so they can become architects of their environment and discover how to lead and succeed as well as show others how.

Through lived experiences, Cathy shows people (not tells or teaches), how they can bring about the change they want to see for themselves. There is impact in the way she approaches the art of sharing knowledge, but before she begins that road map, she pauses to listen so she can understand your journey and where you want to be.

If you have ever wanted to dream big but held back, today is the day you will want to leap forward, as working with Cathy will inspire you to think limitlessly and identify who you will bring on the journey with you.

**'When we rise, it is important to also lift those around us.'**

**– Cathy Dimarchos**

Cathy is a number one bestselling co-author as well as authoring her book, *Same People, Different Vision – Developing Leaders of Today to Shape a Better Tomorrow.*

If you ever wanted to take a chance and do something for yourself, reach out and connect with Cathy. Don't hold yourself back. Turn a dream into your lived life.

Email: info@solutions2you.com.au
Website : www.solutions2you.com.au
FB: www.facebook.com/CathyDimarchosCoachSpeaker
Instagram: www.instagram.com/solutions2you_consulting
Linkedin: www.linkedin.com/company/solutions2you-pty-ltd

# TOP TAKEAWAYS

- Choices when considered and thought-out can lead to opportunities.

- A personal journey may be self-fulfilling but will be left unnoticed if it is alone. A shared journey creates impact and will survive us all.

- We do not need to see the impact of what we do for it to be real, we simply need to believe that by doing it, we are creating it.

# DISCOVERING MY AUTHENTICITY

*Gabby Lambkin*

If someone had sat me down with a crystal ball 10 years ago and told me I would be a Business & Career Coach specialising in Astrology, I would have looked at them sideways! It wasn't that I wasn't familiar with training and coaching business and lifestyle skills. I had travelled the world, working in various roles in community health, and in later years, supported and managed several small businesses. But, I would have baulked at the idea of using psychological and predictive Astrology in conjunction with the foundations of traditional life coaching to galvanise my clients to transform.

When I first decided to go down this untraditional coaching path, my initial thoughts were: I'd be so judged; considered an airy-fairy type; how would I explain this to anyone new I met? I'd always had fun from my late teens, often asking someone's Sun sign and sharing the little knowledge I had gained from Australian Astrologer Karen Moregold every week on Good Morning

Australia before I darted off to school. There was an interest, but I only took the information as light-hearted entertainment and I wasn't in an environment that encouraged this type of esoteric language. I was only made aware of the depth and insight that Astrology can provide in one's life and career when a life path twist in my mid 30s took me where I was always destined to go. And that was to actively utilise the future orientated symbolism of Astrology when coaching high functioning clients who want to live their lives beyond mediocrity.

I grew up like most fortunate Australian girls in the 1970s. I had a loving family, nice (and sometimes not-so-nice) brothers, nice (and sometimes not-so-nice) friends, loved 'playing with our family dog', 'going around the world' with my Coca Cola yoyo and creating all sorts of craft, including knitting.

I was the youngest, and only girl, born into a blended family of 5 boys in a small country town in northern New South Wales. The household was often noisy and chaotic with the family off-spring, and our mum often encouraged us to venture outside. I loved riding my bike with its flower seat and basket on the front handlebars. I even remember decorating the spokes with matching streamers for a local parade when I was 9. It was such a highlight to show off my bike! It gave me independence, a sense of freedom, and a chance to keep up with my older brothers.

Meal times saw us shoved in around a booth-style dining table, which gave ample opportunity for my brothers to steal food off each other's plates. In particular, I was often gullible when my oldest brother would get me to look at 'something', then quickly wisp a divine piece of mum's cooking onto his plate. My mum was a great cook. She had an amazing knack for creating really tasty meals that 'spread so far'. One of my favourite memories was our Sunday night roast dinner with 3 vegetables and gravy.

Any of the leftover meat would be used the following night for fritters, which were a big hit in our household.

Being the only girl and the youngest in my family, I would spend much play time on my own, mainly because I didn't have a sister and also because I enjoyed the tranquility of being outside. If I wasn't riding my bike or climbing trees, I would love hanging out on our lush grass near our swings, and lie down and just look up at the clouds. I would imagine what I could see in their formations and believe someone was up there creating the shapes just for me, helping me build out my creativity. There was something about looking up at the sky that fascinated me. Watching the clouds gently move through the ethers, some faster than others, I wondered what lay beyond. I've always believed there was something past the beyond, as I could 'feel' there was more to the world than met the eye. It was a natural part of me to daydream and think about the deeper questions in life. My mum was often confronted with my 'why' questioning, as I had a deep yearning to learn and understand how people, and the world in general, ticked. I was deeply sensitive to all types of undercurrents, which I tried to hide, as my brothers most certainly made fun of me if I was to show any signs of being delicate. Working hard, being busy, and that 'crack-on' attitude, was very much the focus of my childhood conditioning. There was little to no philosophical discussion, with ego and strongly expressed opinions on show, and plenty of banter on who was better than the next.

My personal exterior was all about my passion for sport. I was a naturally gifted sports girl and labelled a 'tom boy'. Sport was no doubt a highlight in my younger years as I kept busy with representing positions at regional and state level in athletics, netball, softball, tennis and in my teen years playing volleyball. My love for the outdoors saw me with a face full of freckles and always on the move. These talents fitted well into a family of boys where competition was at the forefront. Anything that involved a race or playing with a bat and a ball would draw me in like bees to honey. Although I came across as an extrovert, there was a big part of me that was introspective and analytical, although this wasn't encouraged or given much of a chance to shine.

I was around 10 years old when I rose one cold winter's morning to find myself peering into my parents' bedroom. They used to leave their door ajar when they were sleeping which gave me a chance to check in to see if they were still in bed. I loved getting up early when the house was quiet, but I felt something instinctual that morning telling me that one day I was going to look in and not see my mum lying next to my dad. As I stood there looking at my mum, I had a deep sense of sadness overcome me. I turned around and headed straight back into my bedroom and hid under my warm bedcovers and started to cry.

My mum was diagnosed with breast cancer when I was around 4 years old and had been battling with poor health from the effects of the treatment for years. I was a little helper around the home and her resident in-house physiotherapist, by conducting 'the thumps' daily to her back whilst she lay over the edge of her bed. Even though her health declined, my mum never made a big issue of not feeling well. Therefore, I just carried on with my hopes and wishes for the future like a typical little girl. My mum left us for the heavens above at only 53; so very young and with so much more of life to live. There I was at 12, asking so many questions that started with 'why?'

I felt the branches of my teen years had been heavily clipped with losing my mum at the beginning of those influential years. According to child psychologist, Dr Michael Carr-Gregg, at about 13, we start to listen to the preferences of other people. With influences from your mother, your sister, your best friend and others, you can easily drift apart from your alignment and values. It may be the colour of clothing you wear, the type of music you listen to and even the food you prefer to eat. These preferences convey that you are deciding the value of one option over another, all to facilitate social bonding and group membership. It is during this time we have a tendency to lose our authenticity. There is no doubt in my mind, that I lost much of my authenticity during my teen years, as my father went on to remarry and I lost direction of who I was. I just went with the flow of who everyone wanted me to be.

It was during these impressionable teen years that my self-critical attitudes and limiting beliefs were allowed to seed. My academic schooling suffered as a result of the trauma of losing my mum and I developed the eating disorder of bulimia. I experienced a state of dissociation; a coping mechanism of physical and mental disconnection in response to the consistent stress and overwhelm during those years. I felt physically there, yet mentally gone. It was my protective response to losing my mum; the new marriage and additional siblings in the home felt too big for my conscious mind to attend to. My grades suffered from lack of enthusiasm and distraction, yet I managed to scrape through with a pass. I left school carrying the wound that I wasn't worthy of being heard. I believed I was gifted in just sports and physical activities, not 'head smarts'.

I loved the idea of exploring new places and meeting people from different cultures, and went on to complete a Diploma of Travel. I started my career working as a travel consultant in 1991 for one of Australia's largest chains at the time, Harvey World Travel. And, oh boy, did I get a taste of travelling very quickly. I had only worked within the travel industry for less than 3 years and was rewarded with 'travel miles' throughout Australia, Indonesia and to the United Kingdom and Western Europe. I felt a sense of freedom, as if I was given the opportunity to put behind me the trauma of my teen years. I was keen to experience living and working outside of Australia, so with my fledging knowledge and confidence, I set off with my best friend in my early 20s to live and work in the United Kingdom, with dreams of travelling around the world. I felt like a butterfly emerging from her cocoon, experiencing a sense of excitement and new-found freedom.

I went on to hike and ski many mountains, swim in beautiful oceans and fresh water lakes, spent many nights camping under the stars, sought out exhilarating and sometimes hazardous adventures, witnessed magical sunrises and sunsets, and met so many interesting people along the way. I paid my way by working in administrative and waitress positions, as well a Volleyball Camp Counselor during this time.

With the obvious practical yet mundane tasks such as finding and maintaining a job, a place to live, managing and budgeting money, organising and planning my travels, my lessons were plentiful. I was, unknowingly, using my intuition to keep me safe as I travelled to many destinations on my own. When I found myself in a precarious position arriving in Nairobi in the middle of a coup, when a taxi driver took a deliberate wrong turn at 3 am in Durban, and, when almost falling into a manhole while out for a run in St Petersburg, it was that sixth sense, a gut feeling, that kept me out of harm's way. If I took too much time to logically think through those situations, there's no doubt the outcomes would have been different.

My calling for social responsibility was the decision to return home to Australia to resume a 'normal' life. I was in my late 20s, and I had a feeling it was time to stop running and find my feet.

I had no set goals except to find myself a steady paying job back in the travel industry. I was fortunate to land a position with an international travel wholesaler, and it was during this time, I was introduced to self and professional development, conducted through workshops and end of year conferences. These new teachings confronted me to reconsider my responsibilities by assessing my attitudes, habits and goals. I had never been exposed to this type of training before and it opened up a whole new perspective on life and opportunities to transform my mindset.

There are many cycles we experience in our lifetime and in Astrology one of these such cycles is our Saturn Return. It is known to be a noticeable and impactful triggering event. There are usually 2, and if we live long enough, 3 Saturn Returns occurring in our lifetime. The first is around the age of 27-31, the second around the age of 56-60 and the third 84-90 years of age. Each cycle has its own meaning. The first is when a person leaves their youth behind and enters adulthood. In other words, time to grow up and be responsible. The second is about maturity, and the third is about entering the wisdom of old age. When I entered my first Saturn Return, the universe was asking me to step up and take on new responsibilities. Think about if you have been through any of these cycles. What was going on during these periods in your life?

I turned 30 and married 3 weeks later. A few years together and we went on to have 2 beautiful children. The universe was asking me to settle down and take on the responsibilities of raising a family and everything that goes with it.

As simple as it sounds, I was frightened of raising children without my mum, even though I had a supportive partner. My childhood conditioning kicked in with that 'get on with it' attitude and I bolstered my confidence with lots of reading, including a book by Susan Jeffers, *Feel The Fear And Do It Anyway*. Yet, I was to learn all too quickly, that unless an unresolved issue that is deeply ingrained in the unconscious is not dealt with, it can trigger emotional and physical events within the body. In my case, it was postnatal depression and an emotional breakdown caused by stress.

For anyone who has been through therapy, you will understand the emotional and physical pain that can be endured. Digging up memories from the past and sorting through the emotions so they can be processed and rearranged, is exhausting. Being able to tell our 'truth', to tell our story from our prospective, is a form of healing, as our soul yearns for union and connection. If we are unable to do this, our soul is wounded and we begin the process of self-loathing, self-betrayal and indifference. Everyone has some type of childhood trauma and not everyone reacts the same way. It could be anything from physical or emotional abuse or neglect, to bullying and anything in between. Everyone has an alarm system in their body designed to keep them safe from harm. In my case, I had locked away the emotions of abandonment and everything that was layered on top of that from my teen years. I had identified my triggers of depression were related to my worthiness, safety and security, which then went on to affect so many other parts of my character, including my self-esteem.

Once my package of damaged emotions had been unlocked, it was like opening Pandora's box. I went on a mission of self-understanding, not just for myself, but also of others. I explored many of the personality profiling systems available today including the Myer-Briggs Type Indicator, DiSC profiling, Gallup Clifton-Strengths psychological profiling, as well as attending seminars and workshops that supported goal setting and self-development, including training under the great Tony Robbins. My therapy coincided with another major Astrological lifecycle change of Neptune entering Pisces in February 2011; a transit that only occurs every 165 years. It is known for its passage of global spiritual awakening. This meant I could no longer ignore the deepest realms of my subconscious mind and accept the things about myself that I chose to hide for so long. This was searching for philosophical ideas where we ask the bigger questions around our higher purpose, meaning and our validity on this planet. So, I fulfilled my soul's calling and kept exploring, venturing into the world of esoteric traditions and metaphysical practices that focus inwards on human beliefs, spirituality and wellbeing. It was Human Design and Astrology that I was drawn to and where I have focused recent learnings.

*

I like to look at 'going against the grain' as treading your own path; doing something different from the standard way most people would do it. In other words, going against the normal rules and expectations for how 'a thing' is usually done based on your upbringing or the society surrounding you. It's like the red peg that stands out amongst the blue pegs, by being different and unique, anchoring to an authentic standpoint, instead of being a big part of pleasing others. Time and again, research has shown we are constantly being shaped and reshaped by psychological and social forces to suit the status quo, including the influences of our family while growing up. Yet, we can be truly authentic if we use our strengths and work on our weaknesses to give back to our society in a positive way, and become our true self.

Why is it so hard to be authentic? Being honest, genuine and showing your truth, can be very challenging to do in the day-to-day, moment-by-moment aspects of life, career and relationships.

This is why authenticity is testing, as if we speak our truth and go for what we want, we risk being ridiculed, not liked, or upsetting and offending family and friends. Yet, the more we can get in touch with our own personal difficulty in being authentic, the more able and willing we will be to move past whatever it is that stops us from being real.

The first step is to recognise the resistance with compassion, and be prepared to walk our own path and tell our personal truth. I had to find that path, notice where my difficulties were, and work at overcoming them, even when it seemed a long path as I had many twists and turns along the way. The timing had to be right, for me to accept my authenticity.

*The more in harmony you are with the flow of your own existence, the more magical life becomes.*

This could not be any truer for me, as I took many a journey of self-discovery and transformation to discover my treasure within. I had to learn I was enough … and more! I left school with little ambition but to escape my current reality, only to step onto life's conveyor belt of conformity and follow the masses who seemed to be controlled by what came out of the screen in the corner of the room. Thankfully, like the other wonderful authors in this book, I discovered an alternative life, by doing something as simple as putting one foot in front of the other, stepping through the challenges of adversity, and building and honouring my belief system. Going against the grain has brought me fulfilment in all that life has to offer.

*

Anyone who has ever achieved something in life has had challenges and setbacks – because anything that is worth doing is likely to be difficult. Overcoming adversity is a necessary step on the road to fulfilment. One of the first lessons learnt when I first started on the self-development pathway, was about limiting beliefs and how they uncover what is holding you back.

As humans we are great storytellers, mostly featuring ourselves as the prominent role and sometimes starring others. These stories can account for behaviours over long stretches of space and time. They may be fictional or even fantastical in character. For better or worse, stories are a powerful source of self-persuasion, and they are highly internally consistent. It's our tales that hold a powerful sway over our memories, behaviours and even our identities. It was learning about these narratives that supported me in navigating my challenges and obstacles of my negative self-criticism; that I wasn't worthy of being heard and I wasn't enough. I had to change my attitude to my story and rewrite it so it served me, and others, for the better. One of the best tools I have learnt is to develop a growth mindset and to practice positivity, so it naturally allows me to look for answers within. It has helped me gain a different perspective and consult those who can help me overcome hurdles. A fairly recent example is the consolidation of my confidence in public speaking from a six-week masterclass where I chose to take action and consulted with experts. I haven't yet mastered my nerves, but I'm certainly not going to give up now I've started to address this challenge. Additionally, I continue to embrace positive affirmations and pictures on my vision board. I surround myself with others with a growth mindset, being very aware of others who are not on the same growth path. I'm also accountable with my family when exposing any negative self-talk.

Another story I chose to rewrite, was to accept that it's okay to slow down and engage the introspective and analytical part of my nature. This was something I wasn't taught as a child. I had to learn mindfulness where I could maintain a moment-by-moment awareness of my thoughts, feelings, bodily sensations and my surrounding environment. I am a naturally physically active person and carry a high vibration and therefore I had to learn how to channel my energy into a different form. I mix my mindfulness between emotional freedom technique, also known as tapping, and guided meditations, with my ultimate aim in the near future of meditating unaided. If I somehow end up out of routine, my anxiety and restlessness set in and I lose focus on what I can control.

The people we surround ourselves with are our greatest influences. This may be our family, friends and, depending on how much time you spend at work, our colleagues. The peers we choose to spend time with have considerable influence on our lives both personally and professionally. Take the time to examine your values and beliefs (there are many free online assessment tools including a personalised natal Astrology report), as those who share your same standards will be your biggest cheer squad in achieving your goals. Otherwise, engage with a professional coach to help you navigate your trials.

If there's one thing I've learnt, it's that the universe will continue to send you the same problem until you decide to undertake the spiritual lesson and do things differently.

*

One basic concept I like to refer to is the Tree of Life. Just as we all start from conception, a seed that is ready to sprout, we come forward into this life through birth. If we are nurtured and cared for, we develop through our infancy, growing upwards into an immature juvenile. This is our early life, influenced by our family, tribe or culture. If our environment supports us, just like the branches of a tree, we continue to mature and strengthen, growing upwards to the sky, reaching for greater knowledge, wisdom and new experiences. We eventually develop to go into the world, taking a step on the hero's journey towards self-actualisation, individualisation and self-fulfilment. We strive to achieve our legacy, the highest pinnacle of our tree, whether we are conscious of it or not. The Tree of Life is our noble journey that represents our personal development, uniqueness and individual beauty.

We can choose how we embrace the life we want to lead, first by recognising the values, ideals and roles we attached to ourselves as a child. Our conclusions, repeated over time, then establish our beliefs. And we take actions that seem appropriate because they are based on what we believe. Our beliefs affect what we see and what we select from reality, and can lead us to ignore some things altogether. When we act on old, out-dated values and beliefs that are not in alignment with our authentic self, we preclude opportunities to create a new, better personal vibrational alignment going forward. We can take steps to lead the life we deserve by recognising these past patterns. This is how we nurture and fertilise our growth and development of 'our tree'. This is our point of differentiation in our business and career.

*

All practising Astrologers use the timing cycles of the stars to seek answers outside of the traditional, logical realm. An Astrologer charts the position of the stars in the sky to gain insight into human personality, and even draw predictions about the future. Astrology is essentially the study of cycles within cycles. It is the observation of many different and overlapping cycles in the tapestry of a human life, all which occur over different lengths of time. For predictions, an Astrologer will look to the last time an astrological event happened to get a sense of what we can expect. We are not talking about carbon copies or exact replicas; more like common themes.

The reset of 2 very significant planetary cycles commenced in 2020. One being the Great Conjunction and the other, known as the Great Mutation. A Great Conjunction is when the two planets Jupiter and Saturn orbit around the sun, and they appear closest together in the sky. In Astrology, when these planets are aligned, their vibrations blend and work together. Jupiter is associated with growth, optimism, expansion and thirst for new experiences. Whereas, Saturn favours responsibility, maturity, setting limits and boundaries. This conjunction was special, because it occurred in the zodiac of Aquarius, the sign of social change, humanitarian efforts and justice for all. Their alignment speaks to new cycles of government, new faiths, and new ideologies. Due to this alignment being particularly potent, it signified a complete new beginning, meaning that society will get to start from scratch and rethink the approach to freedom, equality, and what it means to care for the common good. However, this journey may seem challenging for each and everyone of us.

This historic conjunction occurred on 21st December, 2020, the beginning not only of a new 20-year cycle, but a shift from the earth element to the air element, known as the Great Mutation for the next 200 years. So, what do these new cycles suggest and how can we prepare to navigate these new energies? Let's take a recap of the past 200 year cycle in the earth elements. Earth signs pertain to the ordinary, everyday world. It is associated with organisation, logic, common sense, and practicality. It is therefore useful in the creation and implementation of governments and businesses. Earth signs value success in a worldly sense, believing that hard work, following the rules and obeying laws, saving money, investing in the land, and providing services or products that others need, will be rewarded. Therefore, the past 200 years, humanity has embarked upon major accomplishments regarding the creation of organised governments with laws that are designed to support safe, orderly, and functional societies. However, as Astrological history has recorded, applying to the end of a cycle, things don't work as well as they did before. The urge for change in society grows. There will be a gradual move away from the materialistic capitalism (an earth sign type of society where private ownership is valued and people are rewarded materially and socially – in terms of status – based on the success of their efforts) to socialism (an air sign type of government where government intervention occurs so that everyone is ideally equal and taken care of regardless of financial status). As I write this piece, there is a global shift with societies redefining community, new ideas and ideologies taking hold due to contending with inequality and injustice, and new political theories and structures are emerging.

Another significant cycle that is also soon to move into the zodiac of Aquarius is the dwarf planet of Pluto, which represents transformation. While Pluto may be small in size, it packs a bigger punch than most other planets in Astrology. It moves very slowly and can take 12 to 30 years to move through just one sign and 248 years to move through the whole zodiac. Because of this, Pluto is called a generational planet and considered extremely potent and powerful.

One way we can see a different world in the future, is to look at the generational cycles and in particular the Pluto cycle occurring from our past. Each generation carries themes, qualities, and aspects. You may be familiar with baby boomers, gen x's, millennial's etc.

Pluto has been in Capricorn since January 2008 – the sign of firm structures, global corporations, monopolies, and the economy.

Pluto is known to empower, warp, distort, corrupt, deconstruct and transform the sign that it transits through. It is those topics of Capricorn that have been going through transformation and forever changed. To give context to this meaning, examples include:

2008 – The largest bankruptcy in US history - Lehman Brothers, the fourth largest bank in the US at the time, marking an end of the firm's 161 year history, sparking a full-blown bank crisis in the US, Europe and large parts of Asia.

2010 and onwards – the biggest retail bankruptcies of the past decade. Long established brands such as Blockbuster Video, Borders Books, Toys R Us, Sears, Payless Shoes to name a few.

2011 – Occupy Wall St – a protest movement that spread from Wall St to worldwide against social and economic inequality, greed, corruption and the undue influence of corporations on government, particularly from the financial services sector.

The list goes on to include the UK withdrawing from the European Union, the revealing of sexual abuse in the Catholic Church, to authority figures such as Bill Cosby and Harvey Weinstein losing their position of power. So, as mentioned, this little planet packs a punch!

We still have a few more years left with Pluto in Capricorn, as the change into Aquarius occurs from January 21 2024 and continues through to March 2043 (19 years). This Aquarian energy is intrinsic to scientific, social and political revolution.

So, what can we expect as Pluto travels through Aquarius? Well, let's review some of the events that happened the last time Pluto was in Aquarius (January – August 1778; December 1778 – February 1798; September – December 1798).

- The moral theory of utilitarianism (which, among other things, posits that everyone's happiness counts equally) is introduced. Free basic education and affordable housing for low-income families are examples of utilitarian policies.

- The French Revolution

- American Revolutionary War

- Start of the first Industrial Revolution

- The first untethered manned hot air balloon flight

- The phenomenon of black holes is first published in a scientific journal

- Benjamin Franklin invents bifocals

- Development of the smallpox vaccine – the first successful vaccine

- Development of the modern telegraph

- The first steamboat is built by Claude de Jouffroy (steam is water in the gas phase – and Aquarius rules gases; additionally, this revolutionized trade and transportation at the time)

- The Treaty of Paris is signed

- The introduction of the metric system

- Mary Wollstonecraft publishes *A Vindication of the Rights of Women* in 1792 (in response to a report to the French National Convention that women should only receive domestic education). This was one of the first times the role of women in modern society was actively challenged.

- The first dental drill is invented

- The first graphite pencils are introduced

The context of how these themes will be brought forward in the 2020s and 2030s are obviously going to be different from the late 1700s, yet more in line with advancements in technology and digital topics, redistribution of powers, a voice given to the masses, and obtaining freedom and liberation. In summary – revolutions, innovations and discoveries.

The predicted developments for this next Pluto in Aquarius cycle will be along these lines of:

- Significant advancements in holograms, nanotechnology, and robotics

- The next industrial revolution

- A wave of political progressivism

- Power struggles around – and new definitions of – intellectual property

- Political revolutions

- The emergence of new mainstream political parties

- Significant developments relating to outer space and space travel

- New technologies that will decrease our dependence on oil (and will spearhead ecological breakthroughs)

- Decentralisation of traditional power paradigms as those who have been oppressed gain more equality and power

- Technologies we currently could not comprehend

- Major advances in epigenetics and nutrigenomics

Children born during this cycle will be echoing 'equality, liberty and fraternity'. With the state of our environment and life on Earth under threat from a range of human activities, this generation will want to shake up the foundations of the global community. We will see a surge of new ideas from groups and communities confronting power, or those they perceive as threatening their survival and free-expression. They will rise up against entrenched powerful leaders, political powers and institutions that have sought to control and manipulate the populace. New scientific discoveries that revolutionise the economic system are set to alter the social order, striking a permanent shift in the balance of power.

As with all new generations, we will be seeing a new set of values emerging. This generation will be highly logical, unique and scientific. We have already had a small taster of worldwide changes in science, technology, and space travel but more importantly, we will see profound shifts in civil rights and humanitarianism. The most powerful people will be those who work together and value the lives, feelings, and experiences of others. Governments and systems that have worked against each other in the past will find it easier to find common ground and forge new alliances for the future.

This generation will make leaps and bounds with many new inventions that are futuristic, and of course, will determinedly take the climate and environment into consideration. What will be significantly different is that their first instinct will be to think of what's best for others and what will help us all in the future. Group sharing and linking up in networks to share resources will also be the norm.

How do you feel when reading what the next generation of children will be offering to our world? The children born during these coming years, of course, will not be fully in a position to act upon their energies until they have grown to their mature branches of their tree. However, the collective energies will naturally influence our life, business and careers during this period and to embrace these changes, we need be in alignment of where this generational shift will be going. To do this, we must reflect on our own subliminal values and beliefs due to the patterns set from our own generation. It is worthwhile to take a look at how set we are in our ways and how much control we prefer to have over others. As the egos of the Baby Boomer generation retire, I am of the next generation of Gen X's who have been trained to be comfortable with authority, will work as hard as is needed and believe it is important to have work and life balance.

However, as our more radical generations of Gen Y and Gen Z mature in life, they will be more willing to work in humanity's best interests than in the name of greed, power and control. These digital natives are highly connected quick decision makers and Information Technology will be the new compulsory language we all need to be at least conversational in.

As previously explained, Aquarius is in the element of air. Air represents the capacity to process information and disseminate information intelligently. Due to this generation and period being very science-minded and futuristic, there will be much mental-orientated energy. The vibration of this higher mental energy will be balanced by being in tune with your body and to stay grounded in the present moment. Working with the breath regularly connects the mind with the body and integrates them together. Examples of disciplines that uses breathwork are yoga, meditation and martial arts. However, another discipline that is one of my favourite health routines, and is also beneficial for breathwork is to run. Providing you can maintain slow, rhythmic breathing using both the nose and the mouth, you are also essentially practising breathwork. Controlling one's breathing helps focus the mind, detach oneself from immediate reactions to thoughts, and make it easier to get in touch with one's inner sense of peace and calm.

People generally receive social validation for belonging to readily recognised identity groups. This will shift subtly, but distinctly toward a higher regard for those who have found their niche. As we move into a more radical period, now is the time to generate your leadership skills, creative juices and 'invent'! The universal energies will be on your side as society undergoes a revolutionary transition, but be sure you have the best of interest of society and the Earth in mind.

Human life is at a stage whose characters are impressed with different yearnings and dreams, different ways of seeking change and freedom, and the deepest journey of transformation.

Now is the time to share your new concepts, push society forward and march to the beat of your own drum! Step up and to be a leader in your own right, engage your innate gifts, and leverage this to create benefit and good for others. In other words, discover your authenticity and your soul purpose for this lifetime.

In each person's natal blueprint, we have mathematical positions in the chart that points to our most recent past life, as well as our soul purpose or ultimate journey in this lifetime. These points are referred to as the South and North Node axis. The South Node represents those experiences and qualities that come naturally to us, that are over-developed. Whereas our North Node, also known as our North Star, represents the kinds of experiences that we must work to develop in order to work our karma and to grow spiritually in this lifetime. The South Node can be a point of undoing unless we develop the North Node experiences and qualities. Thus, for myself, I have been consciously working on these 'life lessons' of my North Node to bring increased happiness and fulfillment. The axis in my own natal blueprint is that of Leo to Aquarian energy. Balancing and integrating being visible and brave in the world, and contributing to the collective and humanitarian goals.

Moving away from our South Node can be challenging, as it moves us beyond our comfort zone. We may play a tug-of-war between the North and South Node throughout our lives. If we choose to fall back into our South Node energy, this can be a point of stagnancy. Whereas, if we 'consciously' choose to grow and evolve, we will naturally gravitate towards our North Node energy.

I first learnt about my Nodes, when I was exploring my career alternatives around 8 years ago from an experienced Astrologer. As we covered ground on many parts of my personality archetype, the role of Astrologer was suggested as a career choice. I immediately dismissed the idea as it did not sit comfortably with me. However, what I came to understand over time, is that I had some healing and soul work to embark on first before I could embrace and carry out my North Node energies.

Nothing can really replace a direct experience, and it usually takes multiple experiences and deep understanding in order to change the way we perceive life. Understanding my unique natal blueprint has made a profound impact on my journey in this lifetime. It has given me permission change my story to achieve personal transformation emotionally and spiritually. This honest meeting has taken courage, as I felt I was going against the grain of my upbringing, however it gave me a map of how to navigate this lifetime.

As we move into the dominating age of Aquarius, embrace the eccentric energy that is deeply humanitarian and cause-orientated. This is your golden opportunity to rebel against the status quo and disrupt tradition for the sake of a better future.

**The Aquarius Motto:** I am free to live in my authentic truth and express myself as I please.

So, what are you waiting for? Believe in yourself, follow your dreams and reach for the stars. Go against the grain.

# GABBY LAMBKIN

Gabby Lambkin is a compassionate and multi-disciplinary soul-focused motivator who supports clients to navigate uncertainty within their businesses and careers. A certified Life and Business Coach, Gabby is passionate about helping women to become greatly enriched in all areas of their lives. Underpinning her coaching style, Gabby uses the ancient art and science of Astrology and Human Design to tap into an individual's wisdom and innate blueprint. In this way, she is able to bridge the seen and unseen worlds, and blend strategy and passion in a practical and down to earth manner.

As a Pisces sun sign, Gabby has always believed in leading a life of contribution and service to causes greater than herself. She loves to discover the hidden and mysterious aspects of life and often guides her clients into the uncharted territory of new-found knowledge and self-empowerment. Her powerful intuition, integrated with her ability to quickly shift perspective, provides insights which enable her clients to successfully craft and bring their own ideas to light.

For over 20 years, Gabby worked in community health and wellness roles. Then, following the birth of her 2nd child, she branched out into the entrepreneur's journey, owning and operating several small businesses.

While she is naturally self-driven, disciplined and a logical thinker, a shift in the cycles of time ended up pulling Gabby to the mystical and spiritual side of life. An intense period of emotional peaks and troughs acted as a personal checkpoint, enabling her to access the incredible richness and depth of life. It was at this stage that her passion for Astrology and Human design first developed.

Gabby's life purpose is connected to acquiring and sharing her knowledge of the personal self and the higher self (soul). Her mission is to align her clients with their own unique brand of 'stardust' so they can assume their highest potential in their personal and business lives. She encourages them to explore the possibilities of those realms they dream about but are hesitant to step into.

Gabby lives in Brisbane, Queensland with her husband and 2 teenaged children. She relishes spending her free time in the great outdoors, adventure travel, as well as all things health and fitness.

Email: gabby@zodianacoaching.com
Website: www.zodianacoaching.com
Facebook: zodianacoaching
Instagram: @zodianacoaching
Linkedin: Gabby Lambkin

# TOP TAKEAWAYS

- Listen and talk to your intuition. As an evolved fundamental function to each and every one of us, intuition offers a reduction in overall cognitive load and the ability to respond instantly while providing confidence in our knowledge and decision making. Close your eyes and notice if you can feel something in your belly. Is there a subtle sensation of either well-being or discomfort? What does it feel like being next to a particular person or a given situation? We often override this subtle feeling in our bellies out of shame or conformity, and thereby place ourselves into situations that feel wrong.

- Know They Self from an intellectual, emotional and spiritual perspective. It is your self-knowledge that makes you independent from the influences of others. Knowing who you are and what you stand for gives you a sense of self-confidence and resourcefulness. No matter how small your gift or talent might seem, we each have something special to share that sets us apart from anyone else. Sharing your gifts and working on your challenges are a way to give back to the world, not because we have to, but because it gives others an opportunity to learn, grow and advance in ways they have yet to experience. Embracing your authenticity and following your North Star encourages wholeness and fulfillment, as well as supporting others navigate their life school as well.

- Collaborate with a specialist coach or mentors. A good coach and mentor inspires you, stretches you, connects you, develops your emotional intelligence, opens your mind and most importantly, is not judgemental. They provide a safe space to learn, experiment and ask questions. The growth opportunity is immense and allows you to find your authentic flow.

# THE MAGIC OF YOU

*Helen–Lukundo Chonjo*

I set out to have a conversation with my brother. A conversation that resulted from my thinking aloud about the life my parents have led, and are living. For context, my brother is an introvert, and I am the complete opposite. And so, many a time, I sweep him into a conversation that well, he hadn't really bargained for, but which he ends up engaging in because he is nice, and I leave him with little to no choice. That's a lesson on persuasion for another day.

Both my parents received basic education; my mother maybe by choice and my father, most definitely, by the life he was born into.

My mother is the second born from a family of 10 and was born into a thriving home. Her father, my grandfather, did very well for himself at the time. He was an educated Tanzanian man who completed his higher education in Nairobi, Kenya, through a full government scholarship. Our measure of how well he and the family did was in the fact that my grandmother drove a car when my parents were growing up. Now that was a big deal in Arusha, where they lived. So, picture being born of this man and having all opportunities laid down for you, but instead, choosing your own path, one that involved settling with a Christian man (my mother was a Muslim) who was straight from the village and for the most part, being a stay-at-home mother. By choice. She could have chosen a different journey, and every time I ask her why she didn't, her response is always the same. That, she simply went with the flow of who she knew herself to be, unapologetically leaning into who she is.

My father on the other hand, is the fifth born in a family of 8 and the only one of the 8 children who was brought up in the village by his grandmother. *I still don't know how this came to be.* He came to Arusha town from the village in his 20s, at a time when his peers were thriving, while he did not have a single pillar to bank on the possibility of financial security, let alone success.

Despite their differences, what this lady and gentleman had in common was their limited exposure. Logically, the scope of how they understood life, family and success was expected to be limited by their personal experiences. I narrowed it to family and parenting, 'So how did they manage to raise us so differently?', I asked my brother. "What they did with us was nothing they had seen before and was uncommon where we grew up. How then could they have wanted this for us? They hadn't ever seen it done before,' I insisted. In my books, they navigated this parenting thing pretty differently. And I must say, I think they did a pretty good job. I mean, we turned out okay. Maybe even great.

But wasn't this, that *going against the grain* thing? My mother, a nurturer, who let herself be a nurturer, when she could have chosen what society might consider a better choice and purpose with the options she had available. And a man who knew only to fend for himself: a young man with zero resources and a limited connection to his family, giving us a father we look up to today, doing all that was needed to ensure we felt protected, and live a happy, comfortable life. That was not the norm back then, and in some places today, it's not the norm now.

I guess what I am saying is, I never knew how not to *go against the grain*. This way of life was hardwired by the generations before me. From my grandparents to my parents, the first few people I knew and trusted early in life; through how they lived their lives, they all were teaching me to surge forward and live a life of an authentic self. I did not always know this because it wasn't labeled as such, and at no point did we have a family discussion about it. I learnt it subconsciously from watching them do it. And let me tell you, many a time it got me into so much trouble; as I made friends and wanted to fit in, as I became a teenager and craved attention from others, as I became an employee and wanted to climb the corporate ladder, as I became a wife and a mother. In all these instances, I did not know how to undo this part of me and it has been my greatest gift so far.

I am a Tanzania Chagga lady, born and raised in Arusha region. Arusha is located on the northern part of the country, home to the famous Maasai tribe you may have heard about.

I don't remember explicit details about my childhood and even early teenage life. Maybe I took matters lightly, but I do remember a few things; I remember habits. I remember not being afraid to stand out or be singled out for my choices. I was given the ability to make my own choices at a very young age. My parents only ever reasoned with me. I don't even remember having rules. I mostly had recommendations and consequences that were outlined for me, so I could understand the full extent of my actions. Then I had love; lots and lots of love.

My parents were business people. My mother helped my father out when she wasn't taking care of us. They have had several business ventures and worked hard to stay afloat. Because of this, they had a different vision of what they wanted for me. With limited education, navigating through business and entrepreneurship was twice as hard.

But they had a plan to keep my brother and I from all the hurdles of entrepreneurship. To give us the best education possible. Then to ensure we performed well and have our chance in the corporate world, where they saw their peers thrive while they struggled with their businesses. In their eyes, this was a guaranteed ticket to success for us. For the most part the plan worked. I performed well in class and got into the best schools. I even landed my first job after just 2 back-to-back interviews.

What they didn't anticipate is that I learnt more from seeing them live their life and I did not know how to 'do' life any other way. I saw how they stood out and followed their path relentlessly, with utmost perseverance. I saw how it brought them joy and freedom. I was determined to do life that way, my own way. But did I know what that meant? No. All I knew was I had an internal compass and I had to follow it. Like they did. Not to live their life, but mine and to do so while allowing myself the permission to be different from them and from others. The most amazing things happen when I listen to this internal compass. Some call it instincts and others call it gut feeling and may other similar vocabulary. This internal compass will lead you towards you. Take my journey to entrepreneurship as an example.

After university, I was employed in an insurance broking firm where I worked as an insurance broker. I enjoyed my first year of work. I had just finished my IT studies and knew nothing about insurance. This excited me. I had something new to learn, and I was hungry to grow. I worked very hard, and in one year, I had grasped a considerable amount of knowledge and experience in the sector. Then something unexpected happened; my internal compass started to tick. I started to feel out of place. I began to question my role in society; to question my journey, my purpose and my future. The voice was so loud and I couldn't control it. The thought of entrepreneurship crossed my mind. But how was I going to quit my job and work in my own business? I had previously learnt my lesson on impulsive actions. I had to get myself in check. I created a distraction; I put in an application for a raise or a change in my workstation. When my office left the choice to me, I chose to move back to my hometown, Arusha. 'This shift will surely keep my rumbling mind quiet,' I thought. Well, I only delayed it. My thoughts persisted, but the distraction allowed me time to make sure I was on the right path. Over the coming years, it was reaffirmed; my emotions demanding change every time they came. And when they became too loud again, this time I wasn't going to silence them. I was going to step out and be me. And there started my journey into entrepreneurship.

Transitioning from employment to starting my own business meant I parted ways with job stability and financial security to enter into uncertainty, with 2 children to take care of. But now it means freedom and choice; to be there for what and who matters to me, to impact the world around me, to live an authentic life.

Looking back, most of the lessons on authenticity came from my parents and grandparents. I watched them go after what they wanted, despite the circumstances and the odds that may not have always been in their favor. They surged forward and did it in their own way. They lived and continue to live a life of purpose. And where they failed in some of their endeavors, they learned fast and failed forward.

Speaking of failure, my grandparent's spirit towards failure is one that inspires me to this day. My grandmother refuses to stay idle. She would start a small business and give it all she has, and if it failed, she did not wallow in it. She would think of something else and do that. She wouldn't let anyone sway her despite the possibility of failing again.

My late grandfather was similar. He built several prospering businesses with the same attitude. He did not sit aside and watch when he lost a commercial building he had built to a creditor. He could not afford a lawyer at the time, so he made his own case in court. He persevered to fight for his rights while many people who knew him thought it was crazy and impossible. Today, after over 6 years of litigation, his legacy in that building sits with its rightful owners; his wife and his children.

Overall, I consider myself fortunate to have people in my life who modeled a path of authentic living. People who would share their struggles and obstacles alongside their wins, so I knew to take my own path and do things my way, while knowing that this often comes with a price, but one that was worth the effort. Today, I share parts of my story and journey with the hope to do for you what they did for me; so you may see me and be inspired to embrace you and your amazing journey with all its highs and lows.

*

As I write this book, I am a mother of 2 amazing children, amongst my many other societal titles. I'm a business owner and serial social entrepreneur, a master's degree holder and about to be an author, as well as the founder of one of the most disruptive social impact services within Tanzania.

As you may imagine, this has not always been the case. Take my master's degree journey, for example. The entire journey through it was *going against the grain*. When I applied to study for my Master of Science in Finance and Investment degree, my qualifications were in Information Technology. Before that, in high school, I majored in what we call arts studies, being History, Geography and Language. In Tanzania, to be accepted for either undergraduate or master's degree studies, your immediate educational background matters. Therefore, to study Finance, I had to have a background in either, financial studies, accounting, or bookkeeping – which I did not have! To make matters worse, I got the application information late, which then led me to miss the deadline and turn in a late application. Let's not even get into the details of not being able to afford this course. I did it anyway. I applied and got in, against all the odds.

After my first week of class, I came home confused and frustrated. I was ready to quit. I was the only student in class without a finance background. The lecturers taught using financial jargon and referenced mathematical formulas they expected all of us to know. And everyone else did know, exept me. Everything was too advanced, too quick and I understood absolutely nothing.

With a little faith and encouragement, I was reminded who I was, the journey I had been on, and the challenges I had overcome. I was reminded of what God had taken me through in the previous years and I finally was able to call this fear for what it really was, fear. I then marched forward, determined to complete my commitment and succeed. I made friends who I was able to relate to. I asked for help and gave myself permission to make gradual progress. I checked in and was aware I was navigating on a different wavelength to my classmates. At times this meant I was left behind and had to ask questions others may deem as dumb or irrelevant just so I could keep up. It sometimes meant I had to work harder than I was used to, to drive the point across. Other times it meant I wallowed. But I allowed myself this courtesy of it all.

At the time, I was also pregnant with my second child, working a full-time job and in one of the worst emotional states of my life. But I knew who I was, and I just had to keep walking my journey knowing my graduation day would come. As I embraced myself and my situation, my odds improved. And it came. The then mother of 2 was graduating with merit.

And there is that title, 'mother'. I am still torn between being a mother and an entrepreneur. Oftentimes when I am winning with one title I am losing in the other. When my business is thriving and I have to travel for long durations I am away from my children. I miss scheduled practices, homework, school gatherings; the highs and lows of my children's lives. And when I am dedicating time to spend with them, I'm saying no to assignments and job opportunities that may otherwise grow my business. On a few good days, I manage to balance the 2.

As a single mother, the absence from my children hits different, and as a small business owner, the stakes are high. For the longest time, this resulted in me working long hours and experiencing burnout as I tried to be a supermum and super business owner in the name of showing 'I've got this.' It also made me agitated, and I would catch myself getting upset with my children because of things they should be doing, as children. At work, I struggled to concentrate and get work done.

Seeing this, my parents, brother and friends made a suggestion. My parents suggested they help out with my children as I got through this critical stage of my life and business. My brother lent a helping hand along with my parents. My friends offered to host me at their homes every now and then to ensure my work environment changes and I am more effective at work. Of course, I thought this idea was ridiculous. People have it all together. 'I should be able to do the same,' I thought. I wasn't going to abandon my children to focus on my business. And I wasn't going to close my business to take care of my children.

Fortunately, during the COVID-19 pandemic, I was forced to slow down and check-in. I made peace with what it meant for me to be a mother and being there for my children. I realized this will look different for me. It meant ensuring they are safe, loved and provided for even though I won't always be around. It meant they have access to me, their mother, in the best possible form and at any time they need. For my business, it meant, I am able to accept the contracts I need, so that in the future the business is working well in my absence, and have the freedom to decide where to venture and who to work with. So, I quietly accepted their help and stepped into my own lane. Judging from outside, I may not seem like the 'mother of the year' but for my children it meant they are experiencing the best version of me, better than ever before. They are happier and are flourishing.

For my businesses it meant, we have experienced the most growth we have ever seen since we started. For me personally, it means I am yet again experiencing the freedom and joys of being my authentic self as I navigate through this period in my life, which is what I believe is, yet again, *going against the grain.*

As you may tell from my experiences, I define *going against the grain* as the ability to be and tap into who you truly are as a person despite societal standards, norms and expectations. It means having the freedom to live the same and differently from others; embracing parts of your life that are similar to others around you while accepting and enjoying parts that make you different from everyone else. This is a profound way of living but one that also comes with some challenges.

*

I must admit, challenges are hard for me. My initial mindset towards them is not always the best. It's one of those things I am still working on.

It's the initial hit of a challenge that can keep me down and sets me on a downward spiral, a little like the 7 stages of grief. When a challenge presents itself, my immediate response usually begins with shock. This then quickly spirals towards denial, pain, guilt, anger, bargaining and even mild depression, depending on the extent of the challenge. In most cases, this gives life to the challenge and makes it bigger than it actually is. Then the challenge is a huge mountain that, well, I could never navigate around.

The one hack that I have managed to create to deal with the shock of an obstacle or a challenge is what I call 'call a thing, a thing.' I believe in God and what scripture says about me. Two of my favorite reassuring texts at the moment are Philippians 1:6 and Proverbs 19:21, that give me the confidence to prevail. When you take a moment to affirm who you are in God's eyes and the promises he has made to you that are unchangeable, and then analyze a challenge for what it really is, you realize it is not the end of the world. If you are not Christian, you can do this in your own faith or logic. Once you change the lens towards how you define yourself and the circumstances around the challenge, it's no longer that big of a challenge, it may even be an opportunity. And so, to cut the life out of the downward spiral after the initial shock of an obstacle, 'I call a thing, a thing' and suddenly the time I would spend wallowing from denial to depression, is dissolved and I am on an upward spiral facing the obstacle head-on.

Even though I struggle with my initial reaction towards obstacles, I have now begun to recognise the pattern, minimizing it and establishing ways I can navigate through them. Once I have made a decision about what has been presented as the challenge, I use faith to start the process of moving forward. This process has shown me that most of my greatest opportunities have originated from what were initially challenges. Take my startup experience as an example.

'You are very smart. Had you stayed employed in the corporate world, you would have climbed the ladder quickly. You would now be earning so much more and probably be in the c-suite right now. I wonder why you are choosing entrepreneurship.' I've heard this phrase framed in several different ways from many people. At the beginning of one of my businesses, it contributed to me losing clients and almost losing faith in the journey. People were offering me jobs instead of contracts for my business and I needed the money. They were somehow waiting for me to come out of dreamland and get back on the employment ring. While I can't blame them, as I was a good employee, I also knew I had a very different vision for myself, one I prayed over, and one I knew that God had put me here to fulfill.

I learnt through this process not to take things personally and as I called this challenge for what it was 'a temporary setback', I realized that all I needed was time. Time to create a buy in; to be recognized and trusted for my work as a businessperson. I pivoted and focused on me and the things I could control; the rest I left to God. I had my time and my skills. I used them to serve whenever I got an opportunity to do so and that built up my business from the inside out until there was no turning back. Today, the business has been successfully running for 4 years.

If you miss anything else, "call a thing, a thing" and watch the challenge dissolve. As you face challenges, you can do what I do or you can do what you do. The goal is to keep moving forward and be assured that you will see better days. Life is a journey.

\*

Speaking of journeys, through my journey, I have also learnt that you can tell me and I will understand. But when you show me, I will understand, implement and never forget. This is what I believe to be the power of 'walking the talk'. As I write this chapter, one of my greatest achievements would be to see the person reading, doing life in their own way and forging forward with their own story. Not because I told them to, but because I showed them by the way I live my life; a life of authenticity.

This for you may mean living a different life. But different from what? Different from your current state of living, if that is living a life of indifference. You know this when you make choices that tear you apart. These may be big painful visible tears, or small, almost negligible ones. But still significant tears that you can't ignore. You know this when you check-in and call out these pain points for what they really are. If you call 'that thing' for what it is, the way forward is always upward progress.

Taking me as an example, before I could define my values and understand the impact they had, there were things I didn't like being a part of my life. My litmus test was knowing that I knew 'what I was not' and what I did not want for myself. At that point it was hard for me to know what I stood for and the viewpoints I supported for my life. But deep-down, what I have always known, and what I guarantee for you, is that you will always know what you are not if you take a moment to check-in with yourself. Begin by asking yourself what you don't want and what doesn't sit well with you. Don't ignore it; this is your compass.

I guess, what I am saying is, you can start living the life you know you are meant to live by eliminating and getting rid of things that don't align with you. Naturally, you will then attract those that do. Authentic living should not be a mythical thing that only a few of us get to experience. We are all born with it. As babies we were at our most authentic. So we have all lived an authentic life at least once and can do it again. Let's work that muscle of surging forward, which mostly means, *going against the grain*. When sharpened, it will make your life so much better and this world a better place because you are in it.

\*

Born and raised in Africa, I have lived a pretty decent life. I was born into a humble home, but my father quickly made a turn-around in his finances after we were born, and we had more than we needed growing up. I was a smart child, so I didn't struggle with school and classes. I can't recall ever having an issue with my self-image. My parents were always what others describe as 'mushy' (showed affection). My life was pretty amazing and I had it all. My parents ensured we were very comfortable and even in difficult times, we felt loved. This was a good thing, but for the most part, kept me out of touch with reality.

I couldn't relate with struggles others faced, be it in primary school, high school, or uni etc. It was worse than failure to relate because I wasn't even conscious of it. I think I was arrogant and rode on a very high horse. I didn't bully anyone, but I had deep-rooted unrealistic beliefs and expectations towards life, myself and others. I believed things like; if you failed, you didn't work hard enough. If you even slightly deviated from the plan, whatever you were doing was an epic failure. I was regarded as the 'best' for so long, I had to be the best at all things. If things were not going perfectly, it was a problem for me. And the classic blame – 'how could you let yourself do this and find yourself in this situation?' The list goes on. In my eyes, the person and their challenge were one.

As soon as I began university, the lessons also began. My parents could not afford for me to go to the university I desired, which they had promised, so I subconsciously rebelled for the first time in my life. I didn't even know what I was doing until later in life. I spiraled down. I quit my law degree classes and enrolled in another university where I barely graduated. I became the most unbearable child. I didn't attend class, missed my exams, shut my parents out, partied beyond reason, and my relationships and grades reflected this on all accounts. Right before I finished my last year at university, I managed to lose my car, a loss that was a big deal for me. This was the last valuable present my dad could afford to buy for me before finances began spiraling downwards.

The journey of this loss led to what I now believe to be my pivot point, one I will tell you about. While at university I found myself in a situation. That day, my friend had gone to the police station seeking help to find me as she had lost money through a mutual friend. It was our final year of university. My grades were already terrible, but still I hoped to graduate. I went to uni on the day clueless of the events about to happen. On seeing her, I rushed towards her to say hello. I was happy to see her. This encounter quickly turned into an arrest and I was at the police station. I could feel the pain in her eyes as she did this, but I knew she had no choice. She had entrusted my friend with her university fees and he was missing with the money. She was raised by a single mum who worked hard to keep her in school. How could she possibly go back and say she had lost her fees?

She knew the other person through me, so it was right that she shifted the obligation to me. What was meant to be a day in class at university turned out to be a grilling session at the police station. I was questioned for hours, and they demanded I tell them where to find our mutual friend. He had a whole set of problems of his own. 'If they brought him in now,' I thought, 'It's definitely over for him.' I had a plan; to say nothing during the questioning but after, find him and make sure he got the money back to my friend so she could pay her fees, sit for her exams and graduate. I soon released the plan was going nowhere. An officer entered the interrogation room and looked at my ID. He recognized my last name. He knew my father and had his direct phone number. He was going to call him and let him know that instead of being in university, I was sitting at the police station. Reality hit and suddenly I was ready to do anything. I quickly committed to pay for the amount taken by our mutual friend even though it wasn't me who had taken it. I signed a document that gave me a short window to deliver the money. I was a student and it was obvious I couldn't come up with the money on my own. My hope was that within that time, my 2 friends would resolve the matter.

That, of course, did not happen and the police came back searching for me at university again. This series of events almost jeopardized my exams and eventually led to the sale of my car, without my parent's consent. I later however graduated and my parents let me off the hook.

Why do I tell this story? Because the friend I talk about is still one of my very close friends today. Our mutual friend is a person I hold no grudge towards. Because of this, I was able to pivot the horrible situation for them and for me. In this turmoil, I stood for what I thought was right for me; to give my friend the chance to graduate, to give my other friend a chance to make things right, to give my parents a chance to see me vulnerable, and to give myself a chance to graduate. I was only able to do this because I did what I thought was right instead of what others suggested would be right for me in that situation. The experience helped me to discover my biggest skill; my ability to be empathetic towards myself and others.

Going through these experiences from a straight 'A' student broke me but gave me an amazing gift. The gift of empathy. I relate to people with more empathy and because of this, I aspire to leave them in a better state than how I find them.

Imagine a world with more empathy. Imagine people with the ability to understand and share the feelings and experiences of others. Where there is empathy, there is kindness. In my world, we are gentle yet accountable. In that world, people are able to be their true authentic selves without judgment.

Although this is a skill learnt mostly through experience, our future generations can adopt it earlier in life, and this is yet another reason why I share my story. Empathy can be taught. Empathy can also be learnt. As I work in my several ventures and as I navigate through this thing called life, I strive to leave others better than I found them, better than I was. I do this by leaving these little nuggets of empathy through my words and actions and hope they are contagious, so that others, you too, will spread these nuggets to our younger generation, and they can learn to become more empathetic, more humble earlier on. Eventually, this allows you to be you and others to be them. My wish is that our future generations are more childlike, more authentic and that they met with empathy as they navigate their life journey in their own unique way, as they *go against the grain.*

# HELEN-LUKUNDO CHONJO

Helen-Lukundo is a multifaceted consultant with a passion for social enterprise. She believes that with the right support, we all can advance to reach our full potential. Highly sought-after for her contributions to business advisory and support, ideation and social development across Africa she a force to be reckoned with as she sets out to bring about advancement.

Her experience spans over a decade where she has worked for and with various multinational organisations, acquiring sharp business skills working across various teams. As a founder of both risk management and tech businesses, she dedicates her time empowering individuals, teams and businesses to be equipped for their success by instilling skills in people, creating operational efficiencies in business and curating industry solutions for social good.

Helen holds a Master of Science in Finance and Investment from Coventry University in England. In 2019, selected amongst 2000 over leaders, she graduated from Drake University attaining a hands-on leadership and business training through the Mandela Washington Fellowship Program (USA) – a flagship program of President Obama's Young African Leaders Initiative (YALI).

Committed to paying it forward, she co-founded BORA International with a goal to offer support Africa's youth that ignites growth within themselves and their communities. There she also serves as a trainer and mentor and has collaborated with Solutions2You to develop future leaders with the Raise the Baseline projects.

A servant leader, Helen is constantly on a mission to use her talents to inspire, support and serve others, leveraging her academic and business acumen to contribute to the lives of many. She actively looks to encourage and support people and businesses in their journey of development; creating paths and opportunities that empower those around her to seize moments that lead to their success.

Linkedin: Helen-Lukundo Chonjo
Website: www.borainternational.co.tz
Email: chonjoh@borainternational.co.tz
Instagram: @Helen_lukundo
Facebook: Helen Lukundo

# TOP TAKEAWAYS

- We are not unique from our experiences. It is the collaborative synergy of a person's whole journey – people and their collective experiences that makes them who they are. Embrace it all.

- In the process of leaning towards your authentic self, you can also start with what doesn't work for you. That too is a route to knowing yourself.

- Be fluid and empathetic in your thinking and be amazed by the uniqueness of everyone's life and purpose. You are part of everyone.

# NAVIGATING A LIFE ALIGNED WITH PURPOSE

*Karen Mc Dermott*

There have been many times in my life when I went against the grain and followed my *knowing* in what I thought was my next 'right step' to get to where I wanted to be, and it has always worked out to be the best decision I have ever made.

When we live through our knowing we can make decisions with unwavering faith that they are aligned with our destiny.

Growing up, I had no real limitations on how curious I could be – I was able to explore and see where I wanted to go in life. I never really knew what I wanted to do as a career, but I knew the essence of the life I wanted to have – and that was one filled with joyful experiences and one that was truly *lived*.

My mother always said to me, when I came to her with a problem as a child – or as an adult, 'Do whatever makes you happy.' So, I make sure to always prioritise happiness. Even when I sat down beside her in our living room, tears flowing from my eyes, to tell her that I, as an 18-year-old girl, was pregnant, there was no judgement. There was only ever support there to tell me that everything would be alright and not to worry. Even though 18-year-old me was scared, there were so many other emotions happening. I was engaged at the time but I hadn't planned on having a child yet. Despite that, I knew that this was going to be one of the best things to ever happen to me in my life. And when I became a mum at 19, it was the most beautiful, wonderful thing ever.

I love being a mum. I'm the eldest of 6 children myself, so I suppose I've always been a mum. I've always been taking care of siblings – making sure everyone is alright at school, ironing the uniforms, doing the dishes.

I think this is what led me to always end up in leadership roles in the jobs I had. I was always the youngest, but with the most senior role, which is bizarre. Despite this, I was never afraid to show up and get results.

So, after my eldest son was born, I was doing shiftwork in a factory. I loved that job – it was productive and community-based – but it was tough. It was only just down the road from home, but leaving my 6-week-old son to go back to work didn't make my heart sing, however I was young and that's what people did in Ireland at the time. I would lift him out of bed in the cold Irish mornings and bring him to my mum's house so she could get him ready for school. When I worked the evening shift, I would lift him out of bed at 10 pm, take him to Mum's house, then bring him back home so he would be in his own bed when he woke up the next morning.

It was a well-paid job – I even got bonuses galore – but there was no work-life balance. This just didn't align with my values.

So instead of staying a lifetime at that job, I decided to go against the grain. I chose to leave because I wanted more for me and my son. I handed in my resignation and signed up for a humanities access course which would lead into a humanities degree with my local university. I studied hard and worked 3 part-time jobs. I was in love with my new-found love of learning! My heart was singing!

When my son was about 7 or 8, I fell in love with someone. I had my 2nd son when my first son was 9. I had to give up a lot to be a mum to him – he was a 24 hours kind of child – but I loved every minute of it.

It was when he was 5 months old that I was thrust into a period of PTSD which lasted 14 months. I really didn't like it, but I understood what was happening because I had worked in a mental health environment for 4 years – so I was pretty blessed in that sense.

I was diagnosed by the manager of the centre but I chose to go against the grain and not use medication to get through it. I chose to just do what I needed to every day. I went inward. You know, I was a very extreme person, but I went inward to do what I knew I needed to do – and that was to just show up, put my energy into being a good mum for my 2 sons and get through this period of my life. I remember having tunnel vision where I couldn't see the peripheral, beautiful magic of the world. I could only see ahead, one day at a time.

I didn't do the crazy things and have the experiences that I was used to having. It was a very dark time in my life. But when it was time for me to come out of there, it shocked me to my core, and I felt all of the feels. I had a double miscarriage which made me just flood with tears for the babies I lost and tears for the previous year I'd lost to PTSD, but it ignited something within me. It gave me a new passion and zest for life.

I gained so many wisdoms and learnt so many things from my

voyage inward for those 14 months. Even though it was hard, it wasn't time wasted. I call it my cocoon period and I emerged like a butterfly.

After this happened, I ended up marrying my partner and we got pregnant again straight away. We also got visas to go to Australia and we moved there when I was 35 weeks pregnant with my rainbow baby.

This was totally against all rationale because we had just built a brand new house in Ireland. But we locked up and hopped on an aeroplane to Australia. From the outside – and even looking back on it now – we probably looked crazy. *You're about to have a baby. You're about to move into the brand new house you built. Why would you jump on a plane and go to Australia for two years?!* All I can say is that I had a deep sense of knowing that it was exactly what I needed to be doing at that time.

When we came to Australia, it was like a clean slate, like this new opportunity where I could choose to be anything. I was pregnant with my 3rd child, my 1st daughter, and I had the intention of being the best mum I could be and set up a beautiful home for all my children. After 2 years, our plan was to reassess where we were at and if we wanted to stay in Australia.

Since I am not an idle person, I started to write little stories for my kids. I was home all day and the creative juices were just flowing out of me. I became Mama Mac and created children's books. The 1st was about Australian animals, because of course, my children didn't yet understand red-back spiders and venomous snakes. I wrote this book to help explain it to them in a fun way, and I would make up songs to go along with it. I also drew all the pictures for them. It was our special thing and we all loved it.

I still have a box with all the books I made for them. I printed out the pages and coloured them in and stapled them together into books.

This was the catalyst that would eventually lead me into publishing.

In 2010, just 4 weeks after I had my 4th child, I had an epiphany, and the it came from watching a TV show where Whoopi Goldberg told someone that their miscarriage was a visitor that came to help them back onto the right track in life. And if they listened, their gift would come.

This hit me like nothing else.

The call to write a book became really loud, which was totally irrational because I wasn't that great at English in school. I came across the NaNoWriMo writing challenge, which is to write 50,000 words of a novel in 30 days. I decided to accept the challenge.

So for the next 30 days I wrote 1,667 words a day – whilst breastfeeding my 4th child. With one hand I would hold her, with the other hand I would type. And this novel came to be *The Visitor.*

I went on to publish the novel but I just wasn't satisfied with the result or the experience. I was so disappointed – this wasn't what I wanted for my novel. But, from every negative situation is the potential for a positive outcome.

So I thought on that. I felt into it. And I realised that I had learned a lot about the publishing process. I did some further research. I discovered that the print and distribution channel that my publisher used in the US had just opened up an office in Melbourne.

I made a sacred promise to myself that if I became a publisher, I would help stories get told. And I have been doing that ever since. I've helped over 400 authors get out into the world. It's been a real privilege to join them on their journeys.

Going against the grain for me means just honouring the next step, because quite often the next step is against the majority and conventional thinking. It requires you to expand your mind, expand your horizons just that little bit more, which is very special indeed. I cannot wait to see where my journey is still to take me, because anything can be possible. I continue to go against the grain because that's where life is so exciting. You just feel like you're on the right path for you. I have always honoured what I felt aligned with.

I have shown my kids to honour what they feel is right, because if we go against that, we're going against our values. And when we go against those, we go against everything that we stand for. It's just so important in life, in business and everything that you open your mind to, that you go with what the next step is for you, without the influence of others.

I get inspired by people, but I always walk my own path. I don't see any limitations at all. If somebody tells me that I can't do something, I find a way – because where there's a will, there's always a way.

One of the biggest things that came from me opening up my mindset is my writers' retreat in Ireland. In 2017, I hired a castle and brought a load of Australian authors there for a retreat. Who does that? Who hires a castle? What mum of 6 goes and hires a castle in Ireland?!

There were 2 wins in this situation. I was getting home to Ireland to hang out with my family for 5 weeks and just take 5 days out to do the retreat, which was wonderful.

It was an incredible experience to connect with all those people in the castle. We created memories that will stay with each of us forever.

That is why I strongly urge anyone who is thinking about doing things differently – going against the grain – that when you honour your next step, you are inevitably saying *yes* to life. You are changing the trajectory of your future generations. You're leaving a legacy for others to follow in your footsteps.

It's okay to do things differently. It's okay to do things your own way. Because when your values align, success is inevitable. And don't let anyone tell you otherwise.

\*

I go against the grain every day. I do things my own way and I don't apologise for it because it's truly connected to who I am and who I need to be. I share my knowledge to encourage people to do the same so that they can benefit and make their own choices to change the trajectory of their life.

I believe that I don't step out of my lane. I stay exactly where I need to be. We shouldn't step out of our lanes to accommodate other people, we need to stay there to honour ourselves and the paths we need to take. We can still help people while staying in our own lanes. This is how we can go against the grain.

We can probably help others more when we stay in our lane because in doing that, it means that we're showing others that there are options where you can choose things for yourself. All it takes is a bit of foresight and courage.

\*

I face challenges all the time, constantly, throughout every day. But my perspective on challenges is that challenges are positive – an opportunity to stop and pause, recalibrate, to just see things a bit clearer, make a decision to grow and learn something new. Challenges are not a brick wall in anybody's life.

It's up to *you* how you perceive a challenge. I absolutely know that there are challenges in any period or journey of growth. If you are setting intentions and working towards them, you're going to face challenges because you have to evolve into the person that you need to be. When you receive what it is you want to happen, it feels like the very next step for you. Quite often we set big goals that we think are beyond us. But they're actually only a little bit beyond who we are right now. When we embrace things from that perspective, that's where the magic is and that's where life really kicks off.

*

Future generations need us to share our stories. They need us to share what we learn with each other. Where I'm from in Ireland, if somebody is struggling in your community, everyone rallies around and shares their stories to help them through it. So by sharing your stories, you're helping people to heal and giving them hope.

It also gives them knowledge. I remember my uncle, my granny, my mum and my dad just sharing stories of their experiences of life. I learned through those stories to open my mind to possibilities. So I believe it's vital to share our stories because what those around us need to resonate with will ignite within them.

That can be the catalyst for a huge awakening of the mind in their life, which is really beautiful.

So my biggest tips are to:

1. Share your story when you can

2. Really value what you have experienced in life and know that it is really worth something to somebody else

3. Continue to enjoy life, because when we do that, we are being inspiring leaders for others

\*

My aspiration for the world is for us all to focus on connection and what we each need individually. Because when we choose to be leaders in our own lives and really focus on keeping our cups full, it means we can inspire others to do the same and we are able to give our best to each other. When we give our best to each other, it ripples out any negativity and creates love for each other, fuelled by self-love.

It is this type of energy and vibration that will heal our world from any darkness.

I believe we can change our world by changing the energy we put into it. Pouring into ourselves is a great investment in healing our world. Imagine the ripple effect of 10 people coming together who are all the best versions of themselves. Then imagine the ripple effect of *100* people showing up as the best versions of themselves. It will create a knock-on effect on all the people around them.

I hope that you've enjoyed learning from my story. But let's take this amazing time to consider what it is that we can give to ourselves in this lifetime. What are our needs? Because by fulfilling that, we encourage others to do that for themselves, and then we have the strength and the capacity to help others on their journey. It may change our lives and the lives of future generations.

# KAREN MC DERMOTT

Karen is an award-winning publisher, author, TEDx Speaker and advanced Law of Attraction practitioner.

Author of numerous books across many genres – fiction, motivational, children's and journals – she chooses to lead the way in her authorship generously sharing her philosophies through her writing.

Karen is also a sought-after speaker who shares her knowledge and wisdom on building publishing empires, establishing yourself as a successful author-publisher and book writing.

Having built a highly successful publishing business from scratch, signing major authors, writing over 30 books herself and establishing her own credible brand in the market, Karen has developed strategies and techniques based on tapping into the power of knowing to create your dreams.

Karen is a gifted teacher who inspires others to make magic happen in their lives through her 7 life principles

When time and circumstance align, magic happens.

# TOP TAKEAWAYS

- Know that you choose what you want  to experience from your life, so go out their and experience it. Life is for living.

- When time and circumstance align, thats when the magic of life is felt, align that with your values and you will always experience the best version of your life.

- Enjoy the journey, when you experience joy in every moment you will never fail.

# THERE IS UNITY IN DIFFERENCES

*Nicole Hague*

At the age of 16, I thought I knew what I wanted. I may have even thought that I knew it all. Now in my late 40s, I recognise that I knew what I didn't want and that is very different to knowing what I do want.

Never in a million years did I believe my experiences in life would bring me to where I am today, but I am absolutely grateful for it and know I am where I'm meant to be.

Nothing in my life has come easy but it's been nowhere near as tough as some of the paths I see in the young people I work with.

As an advocate for young people and a business woman, I don't always get it right, but I know when I put my head on the pillow at night, I can rest knowing I have done my best; I have been honest, truthful and got things done, without looking through the black and white lens of what's been done in the past. I know I have attempted to make someone's life a little bit better.

I am sharing part of my journey, not because it's easy, in fact

I don't think I am ready, but as I have often been reminded, this is not about me; it's about the impact we can have on each other. I would not say I'm courageous, but I trust in what has been presented to me and in the people I have chosen to have in my life. I wanted to let you know that despite heartache, fear and being bullied and scared as a child, I found something inside me; a voice to stand up for those who can't stand up for themselves.

My decisions today are about the impact I can make on the lives of those around me, who cannot find their voice or find a way to stand up for themselves.

When I first started my business, I had 30 families respond to my call out; they could see the considerable impact we wanted to make. That strong response showed me my path was to continue to have a voice for someone else and to show others they could do the same. Those families became my strength and whenever I falter, I rely on their belief in me, to keep surging forward.

I became a foster parent very early in my life, and I remember the constant reminder of 'you are not their family' while knowing we needed to treat the children 'like family'. That has been a dichotomy I have struggled with for more than 28 years.

The system tells us we must behave in a certain way, yet to do that we need to have emotions and to connect. We need to love and they need to feel loved because at the centre of everything these children need what they've never had; genuine connection, trust and a feeling of belonging.

Today, I share my experiences with my team, so they can think about what is written compared to what is reality, so they can be the people they need to be to support those who have fallen through the system, or have become lost. About 95% of what I do is because I care; I allow myself to feel, to hear and to see what is in front me. Yet the system tells me not to get involved.

So once more I find myself fighting with emotion despite the constant reminder I am not 'supposed' to get attached or emotionally involved.

In 28 years, I have never walked away from a child. I want them to know they have someone in their corner, determined to keep fighting for their rights when they feel they have no choice.

As women, we are encouraged to behave in certain ways. We raise a family, a home and we run a business, but if we don't conform to the standards society expects, or conform to a system, we are ostracized.

But I am not a robot. I am an emotive human and it is through emotions that I survive. I draw on emotions such as fear and love to help me do what I do and be who I am. These emotions and challenges allow me to keep pushing forward despite a system that tells me to do the opposite.

As a foster carer, I believe I was in constant trauma. I would sometimes cry in meetings and behave irrationally. But the kids that were involved, they had no choice, they couldn't walk away. That's what kept me fighting. So while I had a choice, I chose to stay with them.

It did not matter that, at times, I may have sounded like a raving lunatic. I wanted to show the children they mattered. The challenges we faced were not like any other family problems.

When I was 28 years old, I had 7 children; 3 were my biological children and I was a foster parent to the other 4. I was studying to be a lawyer with 6 girls and a boy – so not necessarily the easiest of times. I had separated from their father and these children, I know, needed to work through that period with me. I had to step up and make an impact in their lives so they could work through the challenges they were facing in the community and the school system.

I had met the children's father at 16, he was 18 at the time, and we were together until I was 28. He was devoted to his religious beliefs and would go to church with his parents every Saturday night prior to us moving out together and I respected that. I was besotted with him.

At 18, I fell pregnant but lost that child and the loss left me feeling empty. I felt like a failure and knew I wanted to start a family. I fell pregnant again not long after, and we had 3 gorgeous children together. He worked and I stayed home because that is what was expected. I was bored and have always maintained we only lasted so long together because of the children.

When I had my third child, I was unwell after the delivery. I fell into a coma. We lived in NSW at the time. Despite all the services, my beautiful daughter was airlifted to Queensland for pre-natal care, as that was where they had the best support for her. This was such a strange time in my life, as while I was told I was in a coma and unconscious, there were things I can recall.

I remember feeling like my daughter was safe. I can recall hearing the pilot's name. I had a fear of giving birth. I felt an intuition; the feeling we have as women but often can't make sense of it? I know now this feeling is something I need to be conscious of and respect.

In my younger years, I would have dreams that played out in life. I recall having a recurring dream that included my sister. It was about her telling me not to turn the life support machine off. I could never understand it and at the time I thought that if it were me who needed to be on life support, I would not have wanted the machine to keep me alive. It always felt like a strange dream, until I realised it was not strange at all.

That dream was my inner voice; a message attempting to tell me to be more conscious of what I needed to know. The message in that dream was for me and to ensure the machine was not turned off when I slipped into a coma after giving birth. It was my subconscious sharing a message so I would let my sister know there was a shift that needed to happen.

My mother was quite spiritual. She wasn't a church-goer of any religion, but she believed in spiritual energy, so I was always open to that. What I was experiencing in my dreams played out in childbirth. The fear I was sensing leading up to my third birth was real, as it led to me being in a coma for 2 weeks. Those feelings were validated, and even though they could not be substantiated at the time, it was a warning and a message to let my husband know not to turn off the machine despite any previous beliefs I may have held.

More importantly, I was able to recognise the connections we have with one another. Whenever they attempted to bring me out my coma to see if I could manage on my own, I would crash, and the baby's heart would fail 2 minutes later, despite me being in another state and not being there with her.

It is a reminder that when we sense something or feel something, it's so important to acknowledge it, even if there is no logic. Even when we cannot make sense of it, there is a message attempting to tell us something.

This takes me back to a memory I had as a 3-year-old. There was a photo in the family album of a man sitting with my mum in a submarine. It was not my father and I hated it. Every time I saw the photo, I would hide it and then get in trouble for removing it, but for me it just simply did not belong in our family album. I guess in some way it was because it was not my father. But at the age of 30 I found out this man was my biological father. The realisation in not liking the photo triggered another emotion for me and I came to realise that despite knowing who he was, there was a sense of anger around him though what it represented to me was not clear at the time.

Being a woman brings about things that men simply don't experience and for some reason we are told to do things in a way that suppresses how we feel.

Even as a young girl, my inner voice and instincts were real, and a way I was given some insight. I just couldn't understand it.

Going through our menstrual cycle is real. It is different for all of us, but it is real nonetheless. Our feelings may seem irrational, but if you feel something, explore it, regardless of whether you can substantiate it.

We need to know it's okay to express and share these feelings and intuition, even if it doesn't fit into a box or a system. You just need to be who you are and follow your instincts. By acknowledging this, we can help to elevate women and humans in general.

These subconscious feelings were there for me as a young girl and after giving birth to my youngest daughter, I was reminded I needed to recognise them and where possible, act on them.

At times I have stayed silent and at other times I have taken a step up and had a voice. Someone recently said, 'You are a breath of fresh air to speak with. We should all be doing the same thing,' and in that moment, I paused and asked, 'What have I said that is different?'

It was my ability to be able to speak through 'policy'. You see, I believe we need to adapt and be flexible, looking for alternative ways that will actually help those we are there to serve.

As I write this chapter, I am constantly asked, 'Why does it need to be you though, who stands up, steps in, or fights the battle?'

'Why not me?' is what I say. I know this is my calling. This is the direction that I need to go. I'm not sure why at times I feel that enough is not enough. There are some days I feel like I can't get up, and there are others when I can sit back before I go to bed and know I have done exactly what I needed to do.

I believe I learnt at an early age that I needed to stand up for others who could not do what I could. I knew I had the ability to act and to take action. Are you a woman of action? If you get that feeling, don't hold back because society has told you to, and don't hold back because nobody else is stepping forward. Feel your instinct, feel you gut and know that is all you need to believe.

For me, as long as I can lay down at night knowing I've done my best and given my all, I can get up the next day and be able to continue what I do.

When I look back at my life and my childhood, I know my mum did her best. She did some horrible things, but she did her best and I think that knowing that has become my driver. There does not need to be a reason. When I am asked, 'Haven't you done enough?' today my answer is that I will know one day that I've done enough, but until then my purpose is to be a voice for those children who don't, and to be a voice for the people in the system who want to learn to do things differently.

It does not need to make sense to anyone else it just needs to make sense to you.

At the age of 28, I reached a point. I looked at where I was in life and knew I wanted to teach my girls some key messages and my son to respect others. My marriage was no longer one with love and I needed to model the behaviour I wanted them to have, so that they could see what love was. I did not want them to think love was a wife who keeps a house, cleans and cooks. I wanted my son to see he can respect women and that my daughters can be respected.

We tried to live together but I struggled to be who I was. With his family being so religious, it led to certain beliefs and I struggled to be me. I was the devil woman who was in a relationship with their son. I began to realise you cannot devote your life to someone you no longer love. You *can* walk a path that is different to what society tells you, and that is what I did.

I used to ask people, 'How do you love someone so much, have children with them, stay together for 16 years and then become bitter? Why can't you separate and have a relationship without resentment?' I wanted him to be happy and to have someone in his life that would make him happy.

I made a path for my children that involved showing them the value in following your heart, to be respectful and to not hold anger, especially in separation. Sadly, it did not go that way, it did get nasty and ugly, but I continued to move forward.

I rented an empty house and struggled to make ends meet, but I wanted to show my children, all 7 of them, they could be happy in life, by being who you are, to being true to yourself. We had shared custody of the children and, at the time, I was working on speed cameras in NSW.

Some days I was up at 2 am to start my day, and as that role evolved, I was spending more time presenting evidence in court. It was at this stage where my passion for the legal system came to light.

One day, a sheriff shared a story with me. He shared his thoughts on what I was doing and, in that moment, I was so offended. I was mortified and horrified that we, as humans, had so little faith in humanity and such strong biases. He was talking about a youth about to appear in court, and he referenced the youth as someone who was 'one step away from hell'. I looked at the child, seeing someone who needed support and direction to begin to understand what they could do differently to achieve a different outcome.

That incident was followed by another and another and it was then I realised I needed to be more qualified to be able to better support them.

When I finished year 10, I had done some work as a paralegal so this insight allowed me to consider that I could do more by being more. I wanted to be able to stand in a family courtroom and represent these kids, to advocate for them. I wanted to be able to show them they mattered.

Advocacy had become a driver for me from a young age, but I began to have a bigger passion as I came to see more of what I called 'injustice'. There were times I wish I would have just 'shut up' and I know at times I will pay the price, but I cannot stand back and allow people to hide behind a policy that doesn't make sense, or a system that was created in an environment that is no longer relevant. So I stand up and become the voice for the underdog and go against the grain when something is not quite right. I won't stand down from the bullying that occurs in our society.

While I can stand and be strong, there are other times when I crumble. The truth is I am not as strong as people think. I am vulnerable too but when I know I can step up for someone else that needs to be supported, I find an inner strength; I dig deep.

There have been instances, where I have stopped my car and run out to stop a physical fight! Yes, I have had my share of black eyes, but I wont be a person who stands by or walks away if it does not involve me. I will not just walk past and let things go unseen. I know my family wish I could at times, but it's not me, and it just seems to find me.

I think the universe puts people in front of me who need me. It knows who needs my attention so I can present my point of view, especially if I feel I can make a difference in their lives.

It is why I continue my path and why I am sharing my story

because together we can create a greater impact, together we are stronger. I know I can only do what I do because of the people around me. I am forever grateful for the people I am surrounded by. I am grateful for their trust and commitment, and even more so, I am so proud of their contribution in making a difference.

The mental health issues, the suicide and the stress that we see so often in everyone around us is because we don't feel that we have support or that we are connected, that we belong. This is something I want us to recognise and to look at ways we can make a difference.

Let's not minimize how others feel. Let's remove judgment from society. Let's sit in a space of discomfort, and fear and begin to think differently. Let's look at the segregation that prevents people from feeling they belong, that they are strong, and find a way to elevate people. Let's remove ego and the crown that often sits on our head making us believe we are entitled or that we are better than someone else.

I will share with you my vulnerability; I still wear the wounds and the scars of the moments in my life where I have stepped up. I am not sure they will go away, but in those moments, I know I am stronger than the person being bullied or picked on. I am stronger than the person who, in that moment, has lost their way.

So when strangers reached out to help me drive my mission forward, I knew I was on the right path. I am not one to ask for help, but I too get tired. In 2021, once again I cried out for help. I did it because I knew if I did not take that step, all of those who had relied upon me for the past year would be affected too. I realised they had made sacrifices, and I needed to honour them and what we had achieved. I recognised that 35 families would suffer if I did not dig deep, once more, and call out for support.

In these moments, I go inward and ask myself, 'If this was

not you, what would you do to keep fighting? What would you do to make sure you keep going to the final round?' It is in that moment I reflect and say, 'For as long as I have breath in me, I will keep going.' I find the courage, and the strength to surround myself with the right people and keep going forward.

I continually look at the impact we make on others and reflect on what I want for myself. The answer is to keep doing what I'm doing. My purpose is not about self-preservation or justification of self but on ensuring that we, as humans, continue to evolve and look at how we can be better humans.

My pain and injuries will heal, so I set my vulnerabilities to one side to ensure I don't fall into a heap and cry. I listen to what my heart is telling me, in what I can see we are doing to help others, and keep moving forward knowing there is no going back.

As cruel as it may seem at times, the universe brings me one struggle after another. I know they are presented to me because I will be able to deal with them. It is through pain that we grow. The teaching and the lessons allow us to draw something from them we had not been aware of before.

Sometimes the universe gives me something and I ask why, because in that moment I do not have the answer or the ability to help. But then I know I will be given the tools, or the guidance from someone else, and we will do what needs to be done. Whenever you find yourself in a similar situation, know that you may not have all the answers yet, but they will unfold in front of you, just as you need them.

I don't know if it's my beliefs about self-protection, but I do believe I am strong enough to do whatever is given to me. I know I am given as much as I can take. Sometimes, I do say, 'No, not today, I can't,' but I follow that with, 'but maybe when I am stronger.' I try to focus on my power within.

When I look back at the challenges I faced when I separated from my husband, it may have been easier to stay. There were many times I was told to go back, we both were, but I knew I couldn't. It was not the right thing to do.

I watched my mother being abused. She was a shocking role model who stayed in a drug abusive and violent relationship. She had 5 daughters, some of whom have followed in her footsteps. I remember thinking I would never do that to my children. I did not want them to think they should stay in a relationship that was not filled with love. As a child I hid in cupboards and never felt safe.

I want people to know that we all deserve to be respected and to respect ourselves. I want my children to know there is nothing they are not capable of and whatever they have contributed to in life is valuable, and I value them. This is why I have made the choices I have and I will continue to do so.

Believe in yourself and the impact that you can make, despite what society tells you. Go against the grain and do it your way.

\*

When I was working with speed cameras and presenting evidence in court, there was a matter before the court that involved an elderly man, 83 years of age, and his grandson.

This incident still unearths me. This old man lost his license as he was responsible for his car; the car his grandson had taken and driven as an unlicensed driver.

The law states that the person responsible with for the car is the authorized licensed driver and as his grandson did not have a license the magistrate held him accountable for the actions of his grandson. Now I am sure, as you are reading this, you are trying to make logic of what you have just read, but sadly that was the law in NSW. His license revoked.

This elderly man relied on his car for his mobility to get to the chemist, the shops and to have some independence. He had it all removed because we could not see fault with the system. A law that is there to protect people had no leniency to do what was right. Despite my evidence and standing in court justifying the position, the magistrate had no discretion to change the law or to think outside the box.

It was that day I walked away feeling sick to the stomach. I was frowned upon and got into trouble. I was told it was not my job to have an opinion. I was 32 years old.

That day was the day I stepped out into my own lane. I did not want to be at the bottom of the pecking order. That place of despair was where I often felt I was as a foster care parent. There was time when a child in care was diagnosed with bipolar but could not be labeled that until they reached a certain age, and because they were not at a 'legal' age, they could not receive therapeutic treatment. It's moments like these where I have to have a voice. I cannot stand back and accept that because at some point in history someone thought they had considered everything, the same law still needs to apply today despite how illogical it might be.

It is like someone suffocating because they are having an asthma attack and we leave it untreated because we can't, or have not been able, to diagnose it.

Let's not throw a book at people and say read it, let's look at what is in front of us and find a way to solve it. Let's not give people authority but tell them they have no discretion.

*

I often look at challenges through the lens of how my actions will impact others. No matter what I am faced with, how will other's be affected?

I find, in difficult situations, I need to pause. I go home to reflect. I bring people to the table so they can look at things from a different, non-threatening perspective and allow the conversation to flow with what they think needs to happen.

There have been many times when our business became the subject of discussion because of young people living a life with us as a family (remembering I was also a foster parent whilst running a business).

My belief is we need to create a family environment for our foster kids, but the system has different beliefs in what that looks like. Things like their biological family not being able to come to the house for a birthday, like youth not being able to show they appreciate the nurturing environment they are given, and so coming back to help and pay things forward, is not allowed.

For me, it is about creating an environment to have robust discussions and bring things to the table where we can be open and honest, making sure that what needs to happen is considered so we can serve those we are there to serve.

We are all in this system to protect children, not to reduce or manage risk so we can tick a box. We need to collaborate and work as a collective as we are all stewards of our future generation. As governments, departments and as individuals, I ask that we don't hide behind a document. We must not avoid conversations and discussions because we are dealing with young people who deserve to have a life that is better than what they have previously experienced.

The very nurturing and natural emotions we all need, such as empathy and compassion, are what we need to bring to the table, rather than risk.

\*

If there is one thing I would like to share, it would be to let our future generation know how important it is to stay true to you. Just *do you*.

Resistance is a sign you have to keep pushing forward; the bigger the resistance, the bigger the need to keep striving forward. Don't let fear drive you. Dare to be different. Be what you were intended to be. Own your magic.

Bring *you* to the table. If we keep bringing the same things to the table, we will keep seeing what we have seen before.

Know your beauty is in your strength and in your ability to be you.

\*

Through our mistakes we develop. We can't become immune if we don't make mistakes and get back up and try again.

If at times you have to stop, create a crash and a 10 car pile-up (not literally but metaphorically) so that we can stop and change, then do it.

Adaptability is a learning in itself. We all need to adapt to learn, otherwise there will be no progress. Where there is no growth, we will not evolve as people.

Leave judgment behind and allow yourself to keep an open mind. Try to sit in a place where there is no right or wrong.

Be kind. The world needs you to be kind.

I encourage you to look at each other and embrace the differences we have. There is unity in difference. Understand that some things may not work for you but they may work for someone else.

We all need to let go of control. There is power in numbers, so if you can convince or influence others to join you in thinking differently then I would encourage you to share your voice and encourage others to go against the grain and do things their way.

Most of all, I want to share the most valuable of lessons I have learnt. There is nothing I do, that you can't do too. I am not super human. Nor am I super stupid but I am no different to anyone else. If it doesn't feel right then don't accept it. Don't do it. Step outside the box.

Have blind faith. I close my eyes and I know I can walk through it. I may fall, but I will get up. I may freeze in that moment but I will walk through it.

# NICOLE HAGUE

Nicole is an accomplished Entrepreneur who discovered early in life that she wanted to create an impact on young people. As a Foster Care parent for almost 3 decades, her career took many paths including one of becoming a lawyer. Her passion however continued to steer her to the path she has taken now in serving young people by establishing Progressive Youth Care and Consulting, a service provider in Queensland, Australia that offers sustainable solutions that encourage and empower youth to strive for outcomes that will see them form strong connections in the community and break the cycle of homelessness, substance and alcohol abuse.

As a young woman she was able to identify clear boundaries, and set expectations of herself and those around her based on her values of ethics, respect and in acknowledging differences.

Whilst she now leads teams that strive to deliver care and support that others say is unachievable, her trail-blazing vision is to be part of a steering committee that recognises a commitment to sustainable solutions that include collaboration from community, government and the private sector.

There is nothing that is impossible when it comes to care for young people as far as she is concerned and whilst she is solution focused, she has clarity on how important boundaries are and how discipline and routine form the basis of developing new patterns.

As she continues to navigate through the system and local policies, she is in search of like-minded people who are committed and passionate about solving the cause to what is currently seen across all of Brisbane – youth on the streets, lost and unclear of how to get back on track.

Her mission is to bring the right people to table to break the cycle that exist in policy so that there are better options for young people who fall through the cracks that exist in today's society.

If you want to be part of the solution, to collaborate or have an opportunity to listen to Nicole please reach out.

Website: https://www.progressiveyouthcare.com/
Linkedin : https://www.linkedin.com/in/progressive-youth-b621a420b/
Email: nikii@progressiveyouthcare.com

# TOP TAKEAWAYS

- Do you! Remain true to you. Being real brings with it an authenticity and realism to all that we do. Being yourself is what we know best. Strength is drawn from what we do best and no one else can do it better than you! Stay true to you.

- Act with integrity, be kind to yourself, understand your emotions and trust your instincts. Sometimes the ride is crazy, the fear is real. Just take that breathe and do it ... the path will appear with the goal insight.

- Being different is what creates change. If we all walked the same walk we'd all talk the same talk! Don't be afraid to challenge systems processes and thoughts that do not sit well with you. Just because it's the way everyone has been doing it does not mean its right or that theres is not a better way. Be brave enough to challenge even when it feels your challenging alone. I guarantee you aren't alone – the system works hard to hush and silence those they see as a disruptions to their ways. Challenge loud, Challenge fiercely. Speak even when they refuse to listen. Someone is hearing you ... I promise!

# NEVER QUITE FEELING I BELONGED

*Oksana Kukurudza*

G rowing up the youngest of twelve children in a lower middle-class Ukrainian Catholic family in the mid-sized and conservative city of Rochester, New York, USA, I never quite felt I belonged – whether it was in a social circle, church, or at school. I didn't think and feel like an American, nor did I think and feel like a Ukrainian. I just thought like myself. I didn't fit in with my American classmates and I didn't fit in with my Ukrainian church congregants. I didn't see the world in black or white. I never felt the infectious optimism of the American spirit or the dour stoicism of the Ukrainian existence. My world was full of shades of gray – time for optimism, time for cynicism, time for passion and time for stoicism. It was so much so, that for years I rebelled against being pigeon-holed into any group or belief system. What became most important to my core was the freedom to explore options, evolve, grow and change my mind.

Being caught between different cultures had a huge impact

on my life, as did my birth-place as number 12 of 12 children, with 23 years separating oldest from youngest. Having so many brothers and sisters, I naturally learned life lessons early from those who came before me. In some ways I had to grow up fast, being exposed to mature issues at a young age such as infidelity, divorce, bankruptcy, alcohol and drug abuse, child abuse or spousal abuse. In other ways, I grew up sheltered and child-like as I was coddled and doted upon by my older siblings and, compared to them, wanted for nothing. As the youngest, I had to learn the art of diplomacy early as I sought to navigate familial arguments and varying personalities – attempting to be some kind of glue holding things together.

These varying influences during my early years enabled me to navigate different social circles and social networks almost like a chameleon without ever having to commit to membership, with no one the wiser that I wasn't a member. While someone might think the lack of commitment might make me a lost soul, it actually freed me from settling too early so I could explore multiple avenues in determining who I wanted to be without barriers or preconditions.

My search for finding where I belonged has always been the core driver of my life and formulated most of my choices as well as determined my character.

My search for belonging took on a degree of urgency and excitement as I began to research universities in my junior year of secondary school. My instincts told me I needed to move away from home if I was to learn where I belonged, so I began to apply to universities outside of my hometown. Once I started my university visits, I found myself most attracted to schools in larger cities and with a diverse student body from all over the United States and around the globe. I settled on Boston University, in

Boston; the quintessential college town – a campus with one of the highest international populations. I was accepted and enrolled into Boston University's School of Management. I soon settled on an accountancy degree as my college aspirations were very much rooted in pragmatism. Accounting was something that came naturally to me. It was a highly sought-after skill set and a well-paid profession. It would give me the freedom to explore who I wanted to be outside of college and open doors for me to live anywhere and not be constrained by Rochester, NY.

During my freshman year at Boston University, I joined an international business and economics organization. It opened a new world for me and gave me my first real feeling of belonging. The organization was a perfect meld of business, philanthropy and multi-culturalism. Having started on college campuses in Europe after WWII, its mission was to cultivate international understanding by offering paid internships in other countries on an exchange system. I jumped head-first into this organization and began to support my local chapter in Boston while traveling with them globally a few times. I held an officer and President role at Boston University and a regional role as well. I finally met others, both Americans and Internationals, caught between cultures and trying to find themselves. The most fundamental part for all of us was learning we didn't have to declare anything. We could grow, evolve and change and that was just fine. After connecting with other Europeans, one of my most exciting discoveries was understanding that my cynicism came from my Eastern European roots, yet I still had enough infectious optimism so no one would mistake me for European.

Graduating from Boston University, I took advantage of the international organization's internship program and spent 6 months working for a large public accountancy firm in Torino,

Italy. During this exciting time, I not only gained practical skills in independence and self-reliance living in a foreign country, I also learned to appreciate my family at home. Italians are a very welcoming and friendly people, putting ultimate value on their family – something I took for granted and didn't appreciate on my journey to escape and find myself. I discovered part of me in Boston University, and another part of me in Italy, but I ultimately realized a good part of me was left back home and I couldn't discover where I truly belonged without confronting it.

My next stop in self-discovery led me on a 2-year secondment role with the same international accountancy in Kyiv, Ukraine. If I wanted to understand where I belonged, I needed to better understand my family's roots and culture. I moved to Kyiv, Ukraine in January of 1995. Ukraine had only been an independent and non-communist country for 4 years. The 18 months I spent in Ukraine became a formidable time in my life. I wish I could say the search for my roots was bliss – it wasn't. It was painful. It was hard. It was illuminating. Ukraine as a country was going through a difficult transition to capitalism and I was going through a difficult transition myself.

My goals in deciding to live and work in Ukraine were to gain supervisory experience, discover my family roots and culture, while better learning the Ukrainian language. Since Russian was still widely spoken in most of Ukraine, I ended up working in the Western part of the country where the Ukrainian language still dominated and where my parents originated. On the positive side, I did learn some important managerial skills, met my mother's extended family and improved my language skills. On the negative side, I learned first-hand why Ukrainians are so solemnly stoic – life was hard there. I experienced poverty, corruption and insecurity first-hand, and it was hard for it not to rub off on me. With my travel, I was often isolated with few people who understood what it was like for me. I also suffered bullying from a female boss, which was debilitating. After 18 months of feeling isolated and depressed, I quit something for the first time. I always had the mantra that 'what doesn't kill you makes you stronger' – I was wrong. Quitting Ukraine was one of the best decisions I ever made. The situation, while no one's fault individually, was untenable and I realized I needed to leave.

I gained some important perspectives from my time in Ukraine. I understood how Ukrainians, like my parents, could only cope with dour stoicism when faced with such hardships. Those hardships might lead to alcohol abuse and to other abuses. By walking in my parents' shoes, especially my father's, I was able to understand why he drank and why he lashed out. He had a tough life and he struggled to cope. I came home with a new-found belonging and confronted him – not with anger but with love and understanding. When he lashed out at me for the last time, I offered him a hug and kiss. Our relationship was never contentious afterward, and our reconciliation complete.

I found who I was and where I belonged. I was a woman who has some optimism, stoicism, compassion, empathy, passion, independence, cynicism and ambition. And I belonged to the world.

In 2000, I applied and was accepted to Emory University's Goizueta Business School in Atlanta, Georgia, for a Masters in Business Administration. I knew after my undergraduate degree that I would continue my education down the road with an advanced degree. After graduating from Emory, I took a position with a global consultancy and technology firm working out of their Atlanta office. I was a manager in a global consulting practice that focused on solving the business issues of the finance department. It was my every intention to gain a few years consultancy experience and then move back into industry. My attraction to consulting work lay in the project-based nature of the work. I had gotten a taste of project-based work doing audits in the accountancy firm and was keen to return to client-facing professional services. I learned that I enjoyed the work, the clients, and most importantly, the team members and leaders in the firm. I was also able to continue my other passion – travel while consulting.

In my early years with the firm, I was able to find many mentors and peers who supported the work I did and saw potential in me. Those first few years flew by and I realized I wanted to stay on with the firm and make the equivalent of a partner role. My practice at the time had very few women leaders, and it bothered me. From my very early stages in life, it has always been important to have diversity around me, and the lack of diversity in my practice was something I wanted to change. It also happened to be top of mind for my leaders at the time as well. Luckily, I was working with the practice leader when I brought up my idea to start a women's group of high potentials, with social events on rotation with a practice leader. Those events were deemed highly successful as a start because it gave women exposure and a way to connect to our leaders, something not experienced previously. The events program evolved into a 1:1 mentorship between the business leaders and women in the organization who wanted to unleash their potential. The mentors and mentees were matched together randomly and not based on a prior relationship. Therefore, the mentorship program had mixed results as it wasn't able to progress organically as some of the mentoring relationships were forced from the random choosing.

After 6 years at the firm, I was promoted into a leadership role. I was the first woman in 5 years to be promoted to a high level in that practice in North America. After my promotion, I made the case to develop a more structured and permanent program to assist women in our organization to be promoted into leadership. My plan was to take 4-5 of our highest potential senior managers every year, and with a combination of organic (relationship-based matching) leadership mentoring, workshops focused on the attributes and actions that would lead to promotion, and with a goal of promoting just one woman per year, the program was launched. Over a 5-year period, we promoted one woman into a leadership role each and every year. Eventually, the program was disbanded, not due to failure, but to success. We almost had an equal number of women leaders in the practice and excellent mentoring programs, so a special program was no longer warranted.

During this same time, I had successes with my client work, achieving the results I had hoped. I built a sub-practice within the practice – growing a team from nothing to a 20-person team focused on finance strategy. This led me to another promotion and a renewed commitment to consulting.

Over the course of my almost 20 years as a consultant, I've had my triumphs and my perceived failures on different client engagements. I measure my triumphs and failures by whether the client saw the results I had hoped for and if I was influential enough with the client to guide them towards those results. This has led me to think about what makes me successful in my profession? I have heard it often called 'your superpowers'. When I think about what has made me successful in both life and business, it's been the ability to solve problems in unique and unconventional ways, to lead and mentor diverse teams, and to be authentic and honest with my clients. Younger members of my practice like to work with me over and over again. They tell me how much they learn from me, how I nurture their talent and how I respect and acknowledge their opinions and accomplishments.

I believe my 'superpowers' were incubated and developed early in life as I was caught between two cultures. Being influenced by two cultures helped me develop a unique perspective by which to solve problems. My search to find where I belonged led me to learn about and respect other peoples' perspectives and cultures and therefore, form and manage high performing teams of diverse individuals. In finding who I am, and most importantly being honest with myself on who I am, I am able to be authentic and honest with my teams, my leaders, my peers and most importantly – my clients.

During most of my working life to date, I have focused almost entirely on my career, my teams my clients, and my firm. While my career has brought me much joy, tears and fulfillment, I have always wanted a family – specifically a child. For much of my adult life, I wasn't ready to embark on a family because I was too focused on my career or didn't feel financially secure enough to do it on my own. As I reached my 40s, I decided it was time to seriously contemplate having a family, and at 46 started the journey to have a child on my own.

I began by considering my options which included domestic adoption, international adoption, or to carry my own child. I eliminated adoption for various reasons and since I had started this journey late in life, I went to a fertility specialist to help me. We weighed the different options for pregnancy including the more natural IUI (intrauterine insemination) to IVF (invitro insemination). I decided to try IUI with my own eggs and a sperm donor for a year. When the results were disappointing, I searched for an egg donor for IVF. After more months of waiting, an egg donor was identified, and I tried IVF for the first time. With some luck, I was pregnant after my first try and after 9 months in the middle of the COVID-19 pandemic, I gave birth to my baby girl.

She has become my new priority. It's not that I don't care about my work in consultancy. I happen to have a great client project at the moment and renewed passion for my work, but now work is in balance with the priority of raising my child. I have never been happier or more fulfilled in my life both personally and professionally after almost 50 years of life of going against the grain.

*

When I think of what 'going against the grain' means, I think of people who do not take a linear path or have a traditional life; in the words of Robert Frost, 'took the road less traveled by.' They may have taken steps back to take leaps forward. They may have taken risks when no one in their sphere of influence would have. They may be the people you know who can make lemonade out of lemons. They may be the ones who are unafraid to fail because they know if they don't try, there can be no achievement.

When did I realize I was 'going against the grain'? I guess it would have started very early when I realized I didn't belong to a group or culture, but was caught between different cultures. This initially set me on a course of self-doubt, but eventually of self-discovery. Spending a good portion of my childhood, teens and early 20s finding myself, and my voice inherently set me on a non-traditional and non-linear path. I took some risks most would never conceive or have an interest in. For example, I decided to work abroad in a commercial role, not only in a foreign country, but one in the mid-1990s that had only been independent for 4 years, and was undergoing the painful process of transitioning from a communist economic system to a capitalist one. While my own experiences there were painful as well, I came out with a better understanding of who I was, what attributes I had that made me successful, and what attributes could hold me back. I believe I found myself during my time in Ukraine, not only because of my professional experience there but also because it helped me to understand who I was and where I came from, both ethnically and culturally. It was where I realized 'going against the grain' would lead me to a more successful and fulfilling life than taking a conventional path. This has permeated within me ever since.

Another key realization was in thinking about the key influencers who have shaped me. I cannot pin it on a single person. I am a product of my experiences over my life and how I have decided to respond to those experiences. I have always sought out situations and people who are starkly different from me so I could learn more about them and why they think the way they do. My chameleon nature enables me to navigate easily through situations and discussions with people who are different from me. This ultimately helps me to generate my perspective and then contributes to my own identity and essence.

*

Everyone faces challenges and obstacles in life. It's not a cliché to say navigating challenges and obstacles can help you to grow and develop as a person. While I don't necessarily look for challenges to come my way I have learned not to run from them, but to embrace them, whether they are small nuisances or life-changing. When I come upon an obstacle, I usually look for a 'work around' or non-linear path to navigate and overcome that challenge.

For example, while studying accounting at Boston University, I really wanted to work for one of the large accountancy firms. However, I didn't have a high enough grade point average and struggled to be invited to the interviews. I ended up taking a full-time offer back in Rochester for a local company that summer.

However, not one to give up on a goal, I looked for alternate paths. This led me to seeking an international internship with the student organization I belonged to. I was lucky enough to find a 6-month internship with a public accountancy in Italy. In October of that year, I quit my job with the Rochester local company and left home to live in Italy. I remember my father, who only ever worked for three companies since arriving in the United States and believed in linear paths, thought I was making a huge mistake; quitting a job with such a prestigious local firm to take a temporary internship that paid very little. I told him it was something I had to do. There was something inside me telling me I had to take the risk and I stuck with my intuition.

While in Italy, I obtained some critical audit experience and enjoyed living and working abroad. While doing this internship, the Managing Partner of the Torino office sent a referral to the Boston office, which then led me to be hired full-time about 8 months after my peers from University at the same firm. However, since I had the 6-month internship, I had caught up with their level of experience after our first year.

After a year of full-time work in Boston, I quit again for a full-time role with the same firm, but in Kyiv, Ukraine. This time around my father encouraged me and was proud. I think 2 reasons changed his mind: 1) he saw my non-traditional choice to go to Italy reap rewards; and 2) I was going to his homeland to work and find myself.

*

From the time I was in University and a leader within a student organization, I found myself interested in sponsoring and mentoring those younger than me. This has continued throughout my career in public accountancy, finance and consulting. This drive to mentor and mold has taken on new meaning, getting much closer to home as I think about guiding the growth and development of my own 10-month-old daughter. As I think about the future generation, I cannot help but see all of you in my daughter; how I would want her to be treated, what I want for her and how I want her to thrive. So this will be as much a proposal to her as it is to you.

Whether as a mentor, a friend, a supervisor, a peer, a sister or a mother, my role would be to teach what I know, what I have learned in life, and to speak my truth. It is also my role to encourage others to find their voice and to speak their truth, whether it's taking on a conventional path or going against the grain. I would encourage my daughter, as I am encouraging you now, to seek to understand who you are, what your superpowers are, what makes you who you are, what you like to do and what you do not like to do. Take that understanding of yourself and use it to chart your own course, whether if it's in your career, with your family and with your life. I will support you.

If you don't know yet, that's fine too. Figure out what information you need, what experiences you require, the people who can help you, and chart a path of self-discovery. On that journey, you will eventually find yourself and most likely have some interesting experiences along the way.

The most important thing to remember is, if you do feel different from everyone around you and that makes you feel uncomfortable, you are not alone. If you are thinking of going against the grain, you are not alone. We should all learn to support more of the different because the different in us can be our superpower. We should all learn to embrace going against the grain because that can lead us to a different and interesting life. As Robert Frost says in his famous poem, 'I took the road less traveled by and that has made all the difference.'

*

My vision for the world is for it to be a place where young people feel less need to belong to a group, culture, or country and become children of the world. This world would encourage them to be independent, different and chart their own path from a young age. This world would embrace and encourage them to have the courage and the confidence to be different. In my world, not only would the children grow up with the confidence to be different, they would be raised to embrace and respect children of different cultures and backgrounds. They would be encouraged to develop empathy and curiosity for individuals very different from themselves, promoting an atmosphere of learning and cross-sharing. This atmosphere of respect and cross-sharing would foster inclusion and diversity. I'd like to see a world where tribalism and nationalism are marginalized, where there is equal access to resources for learning, growing, developing and cross-pollinating ideas between different genders, colors, sexual identities, creeds and nations.

I'd like to see young people given opportunities to learn and develop who they are, and not be rushed into identification based on gender, color creed, sexual identity or culture. To live in a world where they are given the room to explore with confidence, whether that means traveling early or staying closer to home. I envision a world that supports continuous learning and growth; a world that doesn't expect young people to stay stagnant, but encourages them to be curious, always evolve and be given the opportunity to change their minds.

We have certainly made some strides in these areas over the past 50 years of my life, but we all have more work to do. My vision for the world is an ideal state that may never be realized, but we can aim to get closer. Even from my own experiences, I understand this. As a global society, it's incredibly important for us to have a mindset that encourages us to evolve and know we can change our minds. From my experiences, some of my best friends across the globe come from very different cultural backgrounds, creeds and countries. I like to consider myself an open-minded person who tries to walk in the shoes of others. However, I still find myself confronting cultural norms I grew up with, thinking they were established and settled but later realizing they were more fluid and uncertain.

A good example is our recent reckoning at home over race relations with the Black Lives Matter movement. Having very good friends of colour, I knew an equal playing field did not exist for all colors and creeds in my country. I knew police were more likely to stop and check people of colour. I knew it was harder for people of colour with the same qualifications as me to have the same opportunity. However, I am sad to say it wasn't something top of mind for me as it did not impact me every day. For many, it is their daily life and their daily fear. I am glad we have given the issue the spotlight it deserves. It's made me realize the situation is even worse than I thought. It's made me consider my own actions and thoughts (that may have been prejudices from my youth), and whether I was contributing to solving the problem or being part of the problem. It makes me stop every day and think about my actions, as well as my inaction.

Another good example is the evolving understanding of gender identity and gender fluidity in our society. Once I think I understand it, I learn new things about it. The best thing I can do is be open to learning new norms and try not to judge. I don't think I will never have or develop a prejudice. It is human nature, after all. However, I will try to retain my curiosity, evolve my position and give myself the opportunity to change my mind. This is my wish for our future generation and for my daughter.

The young people of this world have the opportunity to continue to make strides toward this vision of the world. They have grown up with less prejudice, bigotry and tribalism than I have. I would like to see them not fall prey to the nationalism, division and tribalism that has recently crept up in my country, as well as across the globe. I'd like to see them grow up with the confidence to reject peer pressure. To have the confidence not to settle too soon on who they are but to chart their own path of self-discovery. I'd like to see them have the confidence to choose the path that feels right for them, even if it is the more difficult path with risk of failure. I'd like to see them find the place where they belong and not compromise based on what the society of the day tells them to be.

I'd like to see them commit to global inclusion and diversity; to retain an openness of understanding and respect of others different from them. While as a society, we have evolved, we need to continue to push towards rejecting our prejudices and promoting equality. Soon our future generation will own the responsibility to question how much further we need to go and continue to fight for social justice, inclusion and diversity.

I'd like them to mentor and support others in their own paths to self-discovery; for them to teach this to their teams, peers, friends, families and eventually their own children. And lastly and most importantly, I'd like them to respect the conventional whilst striving to always 'go against the grain'.

# OKSANA KUKURUDZA

Oksana Kukurudza is currently a management consultant out of New York, NY working for one of the largest global consulting firms as a Managing Director. Oksana has approximately 30 years of professional experience starting in public accountancy, finance and accounting roles and finally, post an MBA for Gozuieta Business School at Emory University, management consulting. Oksana specializes in advising companies on how to transform their finance functions through new operating models, streamlined processes, intelligent automation, change management and technology solutions. In addition, Oksana focuses her time on coaching and mentoring upcoming leaders and developing highly effective teams. From Oksana's time in consulting, she has authored multiple thought leadership papers on finance post-merger integration, finance operating models and intelligent automation's impacts on the finance function. She has also been cited in articles in the *Journal of Accountancy* and *Global Finance* magazines. Oksana is most proud of the time she was able to work internationally and the number of consultants whom she has helped to rise within the ranks of her firm. She has heard on multiple occasions that she is the person many of her colleagues seek when they are looking for honest and non-sugar-coated feedback and advice. When Oksana is not advising companies or other consultants, she is busy raising her baby daughter Sofia, traveling the globe for fun, scuba diving, hiking, and skiing.

Email: okukurudza@yahoo.com
Linkedin: Oksana M Kukurudza

# TOP TAKEAWAYS

- It's fine to take time to search for who you are and where you belong; beliefs and opinions can evolve.

- It's important to surround yourself with diversity to better support them and to better expand and enrich yourself.

- Be authentic in business and relationships and you will be more successful at both.

# RAISE THE BASELINE PROGRAMS

The **Raise the Baseline** program was established to support and develop future leaders globally with a focus on paying things forward in developing communities and countries. Our programs are designed to enable young people to become co-creators of the future, their own architect, and to help them discover that community is global.

Participants of our programs are from all walks of life, starting as young as 12 years of age through to young adults. We want them to be able to identify the things that they want for themselves and for the world as they step forward leading a life that they deserve. They each have their own vision of what success may look like and we want to encourage them to choose the path that will work for them. This means our role as leaders, parents, teachers, and influencers is to enable them to see their own capabilities and strengths so that they can stay true themselves.

The programs are focused around key milestones in their lives to leverage what they have already experienced and learnt and enable them to continue to grow and be confident with what they have done, where they have come from and most importantly where they want to go.

Having limitless beliefs and the ability to dream is in every child and is what we want to cultivate whilst also developing an entrepreneurial mindset. Careers in the future will require agility, antifragility, and skills that are transferable across the globe so that they can navigate from one job to another and not be tied down to anyone location or pathway.

Theory-based roles will be a thing of the past and the work-force will be in demand of people that can bring their whole self to what they do, who can show they are conscious of themselves and of others and willing to make a global impact. Being able to think limitlessly and to embrace failure as opportunities to learn and grow from the experience are the roots of an entrepreneurial mindset and essential to create, innovate, and be able to find the solutions needed for tomorrow, their future.

Our children are stepping forward into an evolving and rapidly changing environment, one that we are only just beginning to understand. It is important that our actions of today are made to create impact for the future, focusing on survival only is not enough anymore, we need to build and to thrive while taking others with us.

Collaboration and the art of embracing differences form part of the new way of thinking and living so they can be the leaders of tomorrow. Today is about gifting knowledge that we wish we had when we were younger, so that we could be courageous in the way we stepped into the world.

Giving them the things that we all desire most: a sense of

purpose, belonging and the ability to create an impact that is greater than self. We all talk about finding our tribe, this is why our programs are about our children creating the tribe that brings them to a higher vibration. Success for our future generation looks different to ours and their path forward will be different.

Join me in developing our future generation, so that our children can be the architects that reshape a better tomorrow and the leaders that change the world.

If you would like to support your child to be a Leader who creates for impact for tomorrow Register them for one of our programs here: https://solutions2you.com.au/raise-the-baseline-academy

If you are part of a developing community project and would like to talk to us about how we might be able to support young leaders in your community please register your interest here: https://solutions2you.com.au/take-action

If you can help us create impact through government, education departments or policy, grants, communities and connections please connect with us here so we can create a ripple effect: https://www.solutions2you.com.au/donate-to-raise-the-baseline

Printed in Australia
AUHW020847270722
366799AU00003B/3